# 20 Questions to Ask

## Before Selling on eBay

## Lissa McGrath

CAREER
PRESS

THE CAREER PRESS, INC.
Franklin Lakes, NJ

20 QUESTIONS TO ASK BEFORE SELLING ON EBAY

EDITED AND TYPESET BY CHRISTOPHER CAROLEI

Cover design by Lu Rossman/Digi Dog Design

Printed in the U.S.A. by Book-mart Press

To order this title, please call toll-free 1-800-CAREER-1 (NJ and Canada: 201-848-0310) to order using VISA or MasterCard, or for further information on books from Career Press.

The Career Press, Inc., 3 Tice Road, PO Box 687,
Franklin Lakes, NJ 07417
www.careerpress.com

**Library of Congress Cataloging-in-Publication Data**
McGrath, Lissa.
20 questions to ask before selling on eBay / by Lissa McGrath.
p. cm.
ISBN 1-56414-854-8 (paper)
1. eBay (Firm) 2. Internet auctions. I. Title: Twenty questions to ask before selling on eBay. II. Title.

HF5478.M385 2006
658.8'7--dc22

2005045680

# Contents

# Foreword

eBay is the world's largest electronic marketplace. More than 85 million Americans, and 35 million people in 14 other countries, are registered on eBay. When you sell on eBay it is as if you opened a store in a city with 120 million people, except you have no rent, no employees, and you are listed in the ultimate yellow pages. There are more than 1 million items listed on eBay every day, and more than 5 million people have sold something on eBay at one time or another. Additionally, approximately 600,000 sellers make a living selling full-time on eBay.

If you want to sell your old electric guitar, and you put a classified ad in your local paper, it could be seen by as many people as are subscribed to that paper. Putting the same guitar on eBay would expose it to the many millions of people who search for products on eBay every day. Is it any wonder you will usually get a much higher price on eBay than you would selling something locally?

Many new eBay sellers start by selling items from their garage and attic. Almost every eBay full-time seller got started that way. Once those goods are gone, people start going to garage sales and thrift shops to find new goods to sell. Even today there are thousands of sellers who use these places as their primary source of merchandise—although most sellers move into selling merchandise they purchase for resale.

Lissa's book will take you through all of the essential steps to get started selling on eBay. The material is presented in a simple, easy to understand, and logical fashion. Just follow the steps in each of the chapters, and you will be on your way to success on eBay in no time at all.

SKIP MCGRATH

EBAY GOLD POWERSELLER

AUTHOR OF *THE EBAY POWER SELLER'S MANUAL*

# Introduction

I wrote this book for people like my sister. She has experience buying on eBay, but no idea how to sell. Sure, she's read the eBay help files, but they don't tell you what you really need to know—the things that you learn from experience. This is where I come in.

In 20 simple chapters, I'll take you through the three aspects of selling: preparation, creating the listing, and post-auction requirements. In Question 20, I even explain how to set up an eBay business, if you decide to go that route. Along the way, I will give you tips and techniques I have learned over the last six years to help you maximize your profits.

I see no point in suggesting you buy expensive tools and equipment if you only have a few items to sell, particularly since I can show you how to use everyday household items to get results that are just as effective. So, whether you just want to clean out a closet, or you have aspirations of becoming a Power Seller, this is the place to start.

In addition to the information contained in this book, there are many additional resources available on my Website (*www.lissamcgrath.com*) that will compliment the techniques you learn here.

So, if you're ready to start making money on eBay, read on.

# Question 1

# What Equipment Do I Need to Sell on eBay?

One of the biggest reasons eBay sellers fail is lack of preparation and research. In the next seven chapters I will help you get set up for success. This is a very important stage for you as a seller, and we will be referring back to these tips when we work on the actual listing.

If you have purchased something on eBay, you probably already have the only essential equipment for selling on eBay—a computer and an Internet connection.

I could tell you to buy a top of the line computer, a professional Nikon digital camera, and a $200 tabletop photo studio, but although those are great tools for professional eBay sellers, they are not necessary, and there is no point wasting your money if there are low cost (or no cost) alternatives.

Throughout this book, I will show you how to create a professional listing and maximize your profits, without spending hundreds of dollars on computers, cameras, shipping tools, photo studios, and so on.

Still, keep all of your eBay related receipts and record expenses in a Microsoft Excel spreadsheet. Even if you only plan to sell a few items, you will probably find yourself searching out other items to sell (eBay is addictive). If so, you may find it beneficial to file a schedule C (IRS Business Profit and Loss Form) on your taxes. You will want every receipt from day one to deduct as expenses. It also keeps your spending in perspective—small expenses add up.

# Computer and Internet Connection

Having a computer and Internet at home will save you time and frustration. However, you can use the library or a friend's house if there is no other option. If you are working on dial-up (AOL or similar) that is fine. If you decide to develop an eBay business, you will need a faster connection (DSL or Cable), the cost of which is at least partially tax-deductible. Keep in mind, if you get two services from the same company, you will usually get a better deal (for example, cable TV and cable Internet, or phone service and DSL.)

Web accelerators (MSN, AOL, and Net Zero all have versions) can get you a quicker connection than regular dial up, but you will need to disable it before uploading auction pictures, because their compression tools can drastically alter the picture quality.

## eBay Toolbar

If you are a frequent eBay user (buyer or seller), I highly recommend you install the eBay toolbar on your computer.

Scroll to the bottom of the eBay homepage and click on *eBay Toolbar*.

During the download, you will be asked for your eBay and PayPal passwords. You do not have to provide this, but I recommend you do. This allows the Account Guard feature to alert you if you are logging into a site that is not an eBay/PayPal verified site. It's just one more security step.

There are many other features, such as one-click access to My eBay, items you are selling, items you are watching, and so on. It also alerts you if an item you are watching is closing soon. Go to *http://pages.ebay.com/ebay_toolbar/tours* to find out more.

# Organization and Work Space

Keep your work area as neat as possible. Here's a quick tip for instant organization. Get a set of letter trays and use one for each of your family members, and one for your eBay work. Label the eBay trays as follows: pending payment, pending shipping, shipped.

If you come to a cluttered computer desk, simply sort the papers into the correct person's tray and then you can get to work. It takes you from cluttered to organized in about two minutes.

Once I've completed an auction I print out my invoices and put them in the pending payment slot. The invoices move down the trays as I complete each subsequent task. When they reach the shipped tray, I know I just need to post feedback and move them to my filing box (which I keep arranged alphabetically by the buyer's last name).

### Storage Space

You need a storage space for inventory and shipping materials. You can use a closet or shelf for small items, and the garage is a good place (as long as it is not too humid). Choose a location that will be least intrusive to your home, but still easily accessible.

# Digital Cameras

A digital camera will make your job a lot easier, but it is not essential. The advantage to owning a digital camera is the ability to see your pictures instantly and decide if they need to be retaken. However, if you don't have one, please don't rush out and buy one, particularly if you only have a few items to sell and don't have a use for a digital camera outside of eBay.

You can get a photo CD from most major drugstores (like Wal-Mart) with your regular prints for about $2.50. You can also scan the pictures using a flatbed scanner at home, or use in-store photo scanners and put them onto a CD yourself.

If you want to get a digital camera, I will recommend specifications in the chapter on how to take professional photos.

# $Q$*uestion* 2

# How Do I Register as a Seller?

I am assuming you are already registered as a buyer. If not, go to *www.ebay.com*, click on *register* at the top of the screen, and follow the on-screen instructions. It's very simple, and should take no more than five minutes.

## Username

As a seller, your username should be professional, distinctive, and not easily copied. It should also be short, and easy to remember and spell.

If you already have a username, consider it from a buyer's perspective. Is it appropriate for the type of items you are going to be selling? (*SexyKitten* is fine if you plan on selling lingerie, but not if you want to specialize in high-priced electronics.)

### Changing Your Username

To change your username, go to My eBay, and click on *Personal Information* (under My Account on the left side bar). Now click on *Edit* (next to User ID) and change your username.

You will have the changed user ID icon next to your username for the next 30 days.

## When to Register a New Account

If your percentage of positive feedback is 97 percent or lower, I suggest you register a new account. It's hard to be a seller without an established feedback rating, but it's worse if you have multiple negatives.

# Password

eBay uses secure servers to receive, store, and retrieve your information. It is much more likely that someone would guess your password to gain access to your eBay account than hack in through eBay's servers. That is why your password should include letters (lowercase and uppercase) and numbers. *Never* write it down by the computer—particularly if you have children. Even if you put it "somewhere safe," you can bet they will find it, and who knows what you will end up bidding on!

# Is eBay Safe?

No matter what you read in the papers, eBay is as safe a trading environment as any other. Fraud can occur, but there are many safe guards implemented by eBay to protect both buyers and sellers. So long as you use common sense (don't send cash to a seller, never pay for an expensive item with a money order, always request a form of shipping with a tracking number, make sure you verify that a money order is authentic or that a check clears before sending an item, and so on), you will minimize your problems.

## E-mail Phishing

E-mail phishing (also called spoofing) is an e-mail that looks like it came from eBay or PayPal telling you to sign in to your account to revalidate your credit card details, or your account will be suspended. They always have a link that takes you to a page that looks like eBay, but is actually a fake trying to get your username and password, and therefore gain access to your account.

If you ever get an e-mail regarding your account status that looks like it's from eBay, *do not* click on any links in it. Open a new Internet browser window and go to *www.eBay.com.* If eBay needs to contact you urgently, the alert symbol will be next to your username after you sign in (it is a yellow triangle with a red exclamation point inside it). It will say *1 alert* next to it. Click on this link to go directly to your My Messages inbox.

If eBay sends an account message to your e-mail address, that same message will always be in your My Messages box. If it is not there, the message you received via your e-mail is a fake.

If you're still unsure, forward the e-mail to *spoof@eBay.com* and they will let you know if it is genuine. Remember the Account Guard feature of the eBay Toolbar alerts you if you try to log into a non-eBay/PayPal site.

# Completing Seller Registration

Sign in to eBay. You can check the *keep me signed in on this computer unless I sign out* box, which will save you time. However, you should never check this box if you are using a public computer (library, cyber café, and so on), because anyone using the computer after you would have access to your account.

Now click on *Sell* on the top bar, then click the *sell your item* button. You will be prompted to create a seller's account using your credit card and checking account.

Click on *Create Seller's Account.* This will open a new page for your credit card information. This is a secure site, as we discussed earlier. You cannot sell on eBay without putting your credit card and checking account on file.

## Why Does eBay Need Both My Credit Card and Checking Account Details?

eBay needs to verify your identity. When entering into a legal contract with another party, it is very important for both the buyer and seller to know who they are dealing with.

If someone were to fraudulently access your credit card details, they still would not have your banking information, and vice versa, so they would not be able to set up an account with your details. This double-check means eBay can locate any user and hold them accountable for their actions on eBay.

### *Paying Your Fees*

I have never had problem with eBay's security. I authorized them to debit fees from my checking account each month because it saves me time. If you are uneasy about auto-debits, you can choose to pay each month by credit card or PayPal as a one-time transaction, or mail them a check.

# Question 3

# What Should I Sell and for How Much?

On eBay, it doesn't matter if it is a pen or a penthouse, if you promote it properly, it will sell. Look in your closets and garage for appliances in working condition (make sure they are cleaned up and tested before you sell them), children's clothes, prom/formal dresses, collectible items (particularly discontinued lines/items), coins, books, digital cameras, video game consoles and games, and so on. Make a list of possible items as you go, noting their condition (new—still in the box, new—no box, used, damaged, unknown), and the approximate value.

## Hot Tip !

13 out of 15 searches on eBay include a brand-name keyword. So, brand-name items usually get more bids.

Junk does not sell. Think of it like a global garage sale. The good quality items always go first, and you are usually left with the junk at the end. (However, just because something doesn't work, doesn't mean it is junk. For example, a damaged laptop can sell for a decent amount for parts.)

Avoid very large items like furniture. The headache of organizing shipping and ensuring the buyer knows the shipping cost is just not worth it, unless you have a particularly unique or antique item.

If you plan to develop an eBay business and sell a wide variety of items (particularly if you become a Trading Assistant), you should consider signing up for the Terapeak Marketplace Research (*www.terapeak.com*) complete service package. It costs $16.95 per month, but it will do all your research for you. It references three months of eBay auctions to tell you which categories, ending days, and ending times were the most profitable for the items you are looking to sell, and for how much they sold.

If you are just starting out—and you don't want to spend that kind of money—you can do it yourself using a Completed Items Research Form at the end of this book. (You can also download this form from my Website, *www.lissamcgrath.com*.)

# Searching Completed Items

To begin your search, go to the eBay homepage and click on *search*. On the search form, choose keywords that you would use if you were looking for this item as a buyer. Check the box marked *completed listings only*. This will return a listing of all items with your specified keywords that have ended in the last 30 days. Items with the price in *red* did not sell. Those in *green* did sell.

## Completed Items Research Form

Don't panic if you don't know what to look for. Look in detail at the auctions that ended with the highest selling prices. Also, look at the items that didn't sell, or had a low selling price and few bids. You should complete the form for both the successful auctions, and those that were not as successful. This is very important information to have when it comes time to write your auction description, and so on.

## Google Search

Google (*www.google.com*) is a great research tool. It brings up eBay auctions, but also retail and wholesale Websites. You can quickly click through 10 or 20 sites and see what your product sells for in the retail marketplace. Be creative with your keywords, including words like "wholesale," which often bring up discounted retail sites that sell to the public. Online retail companies often offer free shipping, so be sure to factor that into your price.

Knowledge is power. Become as knowledgeable about your product as possible. This will instill confidence in your potential bidders.

# Buying for Resale

Don't purchase items to resell until you have more experience. You will likely have plenty of items accumulated in your home that you neither want, nor need anymore.

### HOT TIP !

*Sell the least expensive items you have first, because buyers are less concerned about buying from an inexperienced seller if the price is low.*

If you do have the cash-flow and want to purchase items, a good way to get into this is through *www.LuxuryBrandsLLC.com*. They offer starter lots of designer clothing and accessories starting at $499.99 and guarantee the total original retail price to be $2000 (you will probably make about $250 profit because of eBay prices). It's a good way to sell some higher-priced items to get you closer to Power Seller status ($1000 gross sales per month for three consecutive months).

# Drop-Shipping

## Advantages

Drop-shippers are both a blessing and a curse. If you find a good one and build a lasting relationship with them, this can be a great business partnership. This is how it is supposed to work:

1. You list the item on eBay.
2. The winning bidder pays you.
3. You pay the drop-shipper wholesale cost and give them the buyer's shipping information.
4. The drop-shipper sends the item directly to the buyer.

The advantage to using a drop-shipper is that you don't have to keep inventory, or pay for merchandise up front. You only pay the drop-shipper after you have sold an item. So, as long as you keep your minimum price above what they charge you for the item, you won't lose money.

## Disadvantages

What happens if the drop-shipper returns your e-mail and says the item is backordered or, even worse, discontinued? Now you have a buyer expecting an item (that they have paid for), and no item to give them. It is *your* feedback on the line, *not* the drop-shippers. Now you have to scramble to find the item elsewhere, or explain the situation to the buyer and refund their money (and risk negative feedback).

You have to be sure the drop-shipper has the item in stock and will ship in a timely manner. Some drop-shippers can take as long as six to eight weeks to ship items. This is not acceptable for an eBay business, where immediate gratification is everything.

While your profit center from drop-shipping is not very high, it is a way to keep selling if you don't have the cash flow to purchase items, and have run out of things of your own to sell.

# $Q$uestion 4

# HOW Will
I Get Paid?

How to get paid is probably the most important question you can ask. A buyer is looking for the fastest way to get the item shipped. You want a low cost method of accepting credit card payment. The answer: PayPal.

## PayPal

You probably already have a personal PayPal account—most eBay users do. It is the single most effective payment method available on eBay. Buyers like it because they get their items quicker. Sellers like it because they are shipping to a verified address, they have Seller Protection included in the fee they pay, and they get paid instantly.

### Seller Protection Policy (SPP)

You must follow PayPal's instructions to the letter to be eligible for charge back protection (when a buyer instructs their credit card company to reverse a charge).

For details, go to *www.PayPal.com*. Just click on the *Security Center* link at the bottom of the page, and then click on *Learn How PayPal Protects You* on the right side of the page.

## Accepting Credit Cards

PayPal allows you to accept credit cards without a merchant credit card account (which usually costs between $20 and $40 monthly, plus a minimum of 2.5 percent on each transaction). PayPal has no monthly fee.

If you have a personal account, your monthly receiving limit is $500, but there are no transaction fees. However, the funds must come from a bank transfer, or an existing PayPal account balance. If your buyer chooses to send a credit card payment through PayPal, you will be required to upgrade to a Premier Account. Then you pay 2.9 percent, plus $0.30 on this and every subsequent PayPal transaction, no matter what the funding source.

Wait until either you hit the $500 a month limit, or a buyer pays using a credit card, before upgrading to a Premier Account. There are no set-up or monthly fees, so even after you upgrade to a Premier Account, you are only paying the transaction fees on items paid for by PayPal.

You cannot pass PayPal fees on to eBay buyers, nor can you require them to pay with bank or existing account balance funds to avoid upgrading to a Premier Account. However, it is a very low cost compared to the alternatives.

## PayPal Verified

Whether you have a personal or Premier Account, you should ensure you are verified before selling anything. This will allow you to insert the PayPal verified logo into your auctions, which is an important step in building your credibility as a seller. To do this you must add your bank account, as a funding source, as well as the credit card already on file. PayPal will make two small deposits to your checking account. When they show up, log into your PayPal account and verify the amounts they deposited. Now you are verified.

## Security

PayPal is as secure as any bank. I had a PayPal account long before they were purchased by eBay, and I have never had a problem with them. As a buyer, it is a much safer way of using your credit card, because the seller never sees your card number. It's a lot safer than putting your credit card details into a online form to make a purchase. This means that as a seller, you *must* offer it as a payment option. Some sellers use PayPal exclusively, but I recommend giving the buyer other options.

# Alternative Payment Methods

As a seller, you should offer alternative forms of payment in case you have a buyer who doesn't want to use PayPal, or is an international buyer where PayPal is not available yet.

## BidPay

The biggest difference between BidPay and PayPal is that the buyer is responsible for the BidPay fees. Honestly, I'm not a big fan of BidPay for U.S. transactions because it takes too long and costs too much. They also don't accept MasterCard as a form of payment. This severely limits their possible users.

| DO THE MATH | | |
| --- | --- | --- |
| Selling Price | BidPay | PayPal |
| $10 | $1.95 | $0.59 |
| $25 | $2.95 | $1.03 |
| $50 | $3.95 | $1.75 |
| $75 | $4.95 | $2.48 |
| $100 | $4.95 | $3.20 |
| $150 | $8.32 | $4.65 |
| $200 | $9.45 | $6.10 |
| $250 | $10.58 | $7.55 |

When paying through BidPay, the buyer pays online at *www.bidpay.com*, then BidPay mails a Western Union Money Order to the seller. If the seller has a BidPay account, they can have the funds deposited into their checking account, but that still takes three working days. BidPay fees are much higher than PayPal, but because the buyer is paying them, you should offer it in your listings.

BidPay is useful for transactions involving a buyer who lives in a country that does not have PayPal. It is much safer and quicker than bank transfers. Also, because it is a money order, which is effectively a cash payment, there is no risk of a charge back.

## Money Orders and Checks

In addition to PayPal and BidPay, you should offer money order, cashier's check, and personal check as payment options. If a buyer sends a personal check for less than $20, you are probably fine to deposit it and mail the item immediately. If there are insufficient funds in the buyer's checking account, he or she will end up paying four times the original cost (through their bank fees and your bank fees), and it's just not worth it.

Having said this, if the amount is more than $20 you will probably want to wait for the check to clear. It usually takes one to three days to clear, so the delay won't be too long. Just make sure to specify your check-holding policy in your listing.

# Question 5

# What Will eBay Charge Me?

In any business you incur fees. eBay is no different. They have very specific fees for different services and options. I have outlined each of them here with examples to make it a little easier to understand.

## Insertion and Final-Value Fees

You are charged an insertion fee for each auction listing. The amount is based upon either your starting price, or the reserve price you set. If the item sells, you are also charged a final-value fee that is based on the selling price of the item. These tables apply to all auctions except eBay Motors, and eBay Stores.

| Insertion Fees | |
|---|---|
| Starting/ Reserve Price | Insertion Fee |
| $0.01 - $0.99 | $0.25 |
| $1.00 - $9.99 | $0.35 |
| $10.00 - $24.99 | $0.60 |
| $25.00 - $49.99 | $1.20 |
| $50.00 - $199.99 | $2.40 |
| $200.00 - $499.99 | $3.60 |
| $500.00 + | $4.80 |

| Final Value Fees | |
|---|---|
| Closing Price | Final Value Fee |
| Item did not sell | No Fee (also possible free relist) |
| $0.01 - $25.00 | 5.25% of the closing price |
| $25.01 - $1,000.00 | $1.31 plus 2.75% of the closing value above $25.00 |
| Over $1,000.01 | $28.12 plus 1.5% of the closing value over $1,000.01 |

Let's consider an example. Andrew had a set of collectible coins and, through his completed item research, he determined that the set should sell for around $70. He started the price low to generate interest, and to get a lower insertion fee. He knew it was a highly collectible item, so he listed the starting price at $24.99, with no reserve. This was the highest amount allowed in the third-level fee bracket. His insertion fee was $0.60.

Because Andrew did his research, created a good title and description, placed his collection in the most visible category, and ended it on a good day, the set sold for $75.

His final-value fee was calculated like this:

Selling price = $75

5.25 percent of the initial $25 = $1.31

2.7 percent of the remaining balance ($50) = $1.38

His total final-value fee is $1.31 plus $1.38 = $2.69

His insertion fee was $0.60.

So, Andrew's total insertion and final value fees are **$3.29**

eBay will give you a total for insertion and optional listing fees before you finalize your auction. However, you will have to estimate the final-value fee, because it is based solely on the final selling price.

# Optional Fees

## Reserve-Price Auction (RPA)

A seller can set a minimum selling price (unknown to the buyer) that is higher than their starting price. This is called a reserve price. It allows the seller to set a low starting price, but still maintain the right not to sell it for less than a certain amount.

| Reserve Fees | |
|---|---|
| Reserve Price | Fee |
| $0.01 - $49.99 | $1.00 |
| $50.00 - $199.99 | $2.00 |
| $200.00 + | 1% of Reserve Price (up to $100) |

For example, Alice is selling a new Prada purse. She knows it is worth more than $250, but she is prepared to accept $175 for it. She doesn't want to list the starting price at $175, because most buyers skip higher priced items, and rarely look at an auction with no bids. To get the first bids, she sets a reserve price of $175, but a starting price of $9.99. Unless the item reaches $175, she is not obligated to sell the purse to the high bidder.

Alice will pay a $2 Reserve Fee, and a $2.40 insertion fee (based on the reserve price, not the starting price). Alice will only be refunded her $2 Reserve Fee if the purse reaches the reserve price. This is to prevent sellers from placing unrealistic reserves on items.

## Buy It Now

I love *Buy It Now*. With it, you can close auctions and earn a decent profit very quickly.

There are two ways to use *Buy It Now*: (1) as a *fixed price auction* or (2) as an option in a single-item bidding auction.

| Buy It Now Fees | |
|---|---|
| Buy It Now Price | Fee |
| $0.01 - $9.99 | $0.05 |
| $10.00 - $24.99 | $0.10 |
| $25.00 - $49.99 | $0.20 |
| $50.00 + | $0.25 |

### Fixed-Price Auction: Single Item

This type of auction has one price: the *Buy It Now* price. There is no starting price and no bidding. The only option for the buyer is to purchase the item for the price listed. Once a buyer does this, the auction is completed and they send payment. If you have a fixed-price auction listed for seven days, a bidder could *Buy It Now* within 20 minutes of the start, and the auction is immediately ended.

To list a single item fixed-price auction you must meet *one* of the following requirements:

➲ You have feedback score of 10. See the number next to your name when you are in My eBay if you are unsure about your feedback score.

➲ ID Verified. This costs $5. (See the chapter on how to build credibility as a seller for more information on this.)

➲ You have a feedback score or five, *and* accept PayPal as a method of payment for the auction.

When using *Buy It Now* in any format, you should always offer PayPal. A buyer who uses the *Buy It Now* option wants the item shipped as soon as possible, so they want to pay instantly. This is good for you, because you can ship the item quickly and make room for something else.

## *Fixed-Price Auction: Multiple items*

If you have more than one identical item to sell, you can list them all in one fixed-price auction. Your *Buy It Now* price is the cost per item. There is no bidding, so when a buyer uses *Buy It Now*, they can send payment immediately—they do not have to wait for the end of the auction. The auction continues to the end of the duration set, or when all items have sold, whichever comes first. Most people who use this option will list a quantity of between 50 and 100 (if they have it) so that the auction will run for as long as possible.

To list a multiple item fixed price auction you must meet *one* of the following requirements:

➲ You have a feedback score of 30, and you have either been a registered eBay user for 14 days or are ID Verified.

➲ You have a feedback score of 15 and accept PayPal as a method of payment for the auction.

## Buy It Now-*Traditional Auction Format*

You can list a *Buy It Now* price within a regular auction in addition to the starting price for the bidding. The buyer then has the choice to either place a bid, or select the *Buy It Now* option and end the auction immediately. If the buyer chooses to place a bid, the *Buy It Now* option will disappear. Now the auction acts just as any other regular auction. If the buyer chooses the *Buy It Now* option, then the auction ends immediately and that person is the winning bidder.

The only instance in which the *Buy It Now* option will not disappear after a first bid is if the auction also has a reserve price. In this case, the *Buy It Now* option will only disappear once the bidding reaches the reserve price. At any time up to that point, a bidder can use the *Buy It Now* option and end the auction, regardless of how many bids have been placed.

To list an auction adding the *Buy It Now* option, you must meet *one* of the following criteria:

- ➲ A feedback score of at least 10.
- ➲ ID verified.
- ➲ A feedback score of five *and* accept PayPal as a method of payment for the auction.

# Listing Upgrades

With so many items listed on eBay, you need to make sure yours is found. A good title is one of the most important things, but there are other options available (for a price) from eBay. On the following page there is a chart showing the costs of some of the available options.

# A Few Words About Featured Auctions

## Gallery Featured

Gallery Featured is a great option. It will give you a bigger picture and place you at the top of the category/search listings. If you are selling a high-priced item, or something that will really sell itself with its picture, I would recommend this option. At $19.95, it is pricey, but worth it if you have a particularly interesting or unique item.

## What Will eBay Charge Me?

| Optional Listing Upgrade Fees | | |
|---|---|---|
| **Item** | **Fee** | **Description** |
| Gallery | $0.35 | Uses your picture and puts it in the "Gallery" where bidders can search primarily by picture. |
| Listing Designer | $0.10 | Helps you layout your auction and use picture themes to make it more appealing |
| Item Subtitle | $0.50 | Allows you to give more information about your item. It is located under your auction title on the search results page. |
| Bold | $1.00 | Makes your main title text bold. Recommended for most items. |
| Scheduled Listings | $0.10 | Sets your listing to post at a certain time. Useful if you are going away, but not worthwhile otherwise. |
| 10-day Duration | $0.40 | An Additional 3 days of listing. Useful for Dutch auctions and multiple quantity *Buy It Now*. Otherwise, don't bother. |
| Gift Services | $0.25 | Inserts a gift icon next to your item title. Some people search by gift items—but generally only worth the expense around the holidays. |
| Border | $3.00 | Puts a dark grey border around your item title, subtitle, and picture in the search results page. No usually worth it unless it's a high-priced item. |
| Highlight | $5.00 | Highlights the background around your title, subtitle, and picture. Good for high-priced items in multiple auction format. |
| Featured Plus! | $19.95 | Puts your item at the top of the search page it would usually be in, and also in the featured section of the category page. |
| Gallery Featured | $19.95 | Makes your picture bigger and positions it in the featured section at the top of the page. |
| Homepage Featured | $39.95 | Gives your item a chance of rotating onto the Homepage Featured section. |
| Homepage Feature (multiple quantity) | $79.95 | Same as previous, but more costly. Only advised for a large quantity of high-priced items. |
| List in 2 categories | Double all fees | List the same auction in 2 categories. Can help increase bids, but costs twice as much in fees. |

## Featured Plus!

Featured Plus! places your item at the top of the page it would normally fall on, *not* at the beginning of all of the search results. The default for displaying search results is "ending soonest." So, if your item matches the bidders search, but you only listed it that same day and it is a seven day auction, your item is going to be on one of the last search pages. If you choose to use this option, it is very important that you consider your ending day and time since that is the only time you are likely to be on the first search results page. Generally, I don't recommend this option. I suggest using highlight, bold, and border, which would cost $9, rather than $19.95 for Featured Plus!

## Homepage Featured

The Homepage Featured option is expensive at $39.95 for a single item, especially with no guarantee that the item will even rotate onto the homepage and if so, what time of the day or night it will be posted. I recommend it only for high-priced items with a 10 day duration (to give you more chance of rotating onto the homepage). It is often worthwhile for multiple item listings if they are all high priced (remember the price increases to $79.95 whether you have two items or 200, so make sure your quantity is as high as possible). Make sure you do test markets within the categories, and make sure there is a market for your items before laying out this kind of money for a feature fee.

As an occasional seller, I don't recommend featuring (other than possibly Gallery Feature) unless you have a particularly expensive, unique, or high-demand item. Look at your expected selling price verses the fees you will need to pay. You will ultimately need to make the decision if it is worth it or not.

# Picture Services

Your title and pictures are the most important tools for a successful auction. You should *always* have at least one picture in your auction (the first one is free anyway).

I will go into detail about techniques for taking pictures in Question 6, but you should log on to eBay to view the fees associated with listing auction photos. From the eBay homepage, click on *The Learning Center* link at the bottom of the page, and then *Selling Overview*. On the right of the screen is a link for *Seller Fees*. Click on this link and the scroll down to view the *eBay Picture Service Fees*. Photos are one of the best areas to spend a bit of money to dramatically increase your auction bids.

## Picture Pack

Remember, when placing an item for auction, you are using photographs as a substitute for the buyer's chance to actually handle the item prior to placing a bid. The more information you can give them, the more comfortable they will be in bidding. They also can't say it wasn't "as described."

If your item should sell for $20 or more, I recommend the six-picture pack. If you have a lot of details to show you may want to consider the 12-picture pack.

These optional listing fees may seem relatively low, but they add up. Consider what will make *your* auction stand out the most, and how much you can afford to spend on fees. Remember, optional fees are not refunded if your item doesn't sell. My recommendation is bold and gallery for every auction, at least one picture, and a subtitle when you have a lot of competition (or you need more space for details to grab bidders' attention).

# Multiple Item (Dutch) Auctions

A Dutch auction is very similar to the fixed-price, multiple item auction, but instead of a *Buy It Now* price, you list a starting price and buyers bid that amount or higher. Your insertion fee is calculated by multiplying the starting price (per item) by the quantity you have for sale. The maximum insertion fee for a Dutch auction is $4.80. Let's look at an example.

Dave has 10 identical Sony digital cameras that he is listing in a Dutch auction, each with a starting price of $150. By multiplying the insertion fee per item by the quantity available, Dave should be paying $24 for his insertion fee ($2.40 × 10). However, because the maximum listing fee for Dutch auctions is $4.80, this is the maximum he will pay. Assuming all 10 items sell, Dave will save himself $19.20 in insertion fees by listing a Dutch auction rather than 10 single item auctions.

As you can see, it is more profitable to sell high-priced items at Dutch auctions than low-priced items.

## Final-Value Fees for Dutch Auctions

The final-value fee for a Dutch auction is calculated by using the lowest successful bid, and multiplying it by the total quantity of items sold in that auction.

Let's look at Dave's digital cameras again. He had 10 items available, and he got 16 bids, listed from highest to lowest:

| | | | |
|---|---|---|---|
| 1. $220 | 5. $195 | 9. $170 | 13. $150 |
| 2. $200 | 6. $180 | 10. $170 | 14. $150 |
| 3. $200 | 7. $180 | 11. $155 | 15. $150 |
| 4. $195 | 8. $175 | 12. $150 | 16. $150 |

Only the top 10 bidders will get the item. It will sell for $170 (the lowest successful bid) to each person regardless of what they actually bid.

Okay, now let's calculate Dave's final-value fee. Look back at the final-value fee table if this is confusing to you.

The cameras selling price ($170) falls within the $25.01 to $1000 bracket, so Dave knows he will have to pay 5.75 percent of the first $25 (which is $1.31), and multiply the remaining balance ($145) by 2.75 percent, (which is $3.99). He adds $3.99 and $1.31 for the total final-value fee of $5.40 per item.

Here's the easiest way to do it. If your item sells for between $25.01 and $1000, immediately deduct $25 from the selling price. Now multiply the remainder by 2.75 percent and add $1.31.

10 cameras sold for $170 each.

5.25 percent of the initial $25.00 ($1.31) *plus* 2.75 percent of the remaining balance ($145 x 2.75 percent) = $3.99.

Final-value fee per item is $1.31 *plus* $3.99 = $5.40.

Total final-value fee (10 items) is $3.99 × 10 = $54.

Dave's total insertion fee is $4.80.

Dave's total listing fees are $58.80.

Now, $58.80 sounds like a lot, but consider that Dave just grossed $1700 ($170 × 10) from one auction.

If less than 10 people bid on the cameras, each bidder would get it for $150 (the minimum bid). Dave's *final value fee* would only be multiplied by the number of items that actually sold. eBay restricts you to 10 identical auctions listed at any one time. With a Dutch auction, you can sell as many identical items as you want within just one auction. If your item is particularly "hot," you can make a lot of money very quickly this way.

# eBay Stores

An eBay store is a page of fixed-price *Buy It Now* auctions, but the rules and fees for a store are completely different. They are useful if you have a lot of inventory—listing fees are cheaper and the auction duration is longer (30 days minimum). While I like eBay stores, at $15.95 a month, you need a lot of successful auctions to make it worthwhile. I don't recommend setting up an eBay store until you have a bit more experience, but I will go into more detail about them in Question 20.

# Question 6

# How Can I Take Professional Photos With My Camera?

You've heard it before, "A picture is worth a thousand words." Well, it's true. Once a potential bidder has clicked on your auction, the first thing they look for is the picture. If they are browsing the gallery, they will be looking at your picture even before looking at your title. So it is vitally important to display the best possible picture you can.

Having said that, you don't need a fancy digital camera or professional studio to get great pictures. Your cheap, five-year old, 1.2 megapixel camera is just fine. You can even use film if you don't have a digital camera.

Jim Salvas (eBay username: camerajim) is a professional photographer. He is also an eBay Power Seller who deals in photography accessories and equipment. He recently conducted two excellent workshops on auction photography techniques on the eBay forums, and has very kindly allowed me to pass on his tips and techniques to you.

Some of these you may know already, others will surprise you. All of them will save you time and money, and help even the complete novice take great pictures in no time.

# Never List an Auction Without a Picture

Would you buy a product you have never seen from a person you have never met? I wouldn't, and neither would most buyers. You must include at least one picture, and list it in the gallery ($0.35), as many buyers search gallery items exclusively. If you have a picture in your auction, but not in the gallery, you won't show up in the picture gallery view.

Your first picture upload is free, and it is definitely worth $0.35 to have it placed in the gallery, no matter what your item is.

Include at least one picture of the actual item you are selling. You can use a stock picture as well, but many buyers think auctions that only use stock photos are trying to hide something wrong with the actual items. This translates to lower and fewer bids. Bidders want to see exactly what they are purchasing. They want close-up images, so they are fully aware of any flaws in advance.

If you only use a stock picture, your buyer is going to expect an item in perfect stock condition. Anything less and he or she will feel like the item was not as described in the listing (and respond with appropriate feedback).

## Copyright and VeRO

During the listing process, eBay may offer a stock picture that has been approved for use by the item's manufacturer. This is okay to use, but you cannot take a picture from the manufacturer's Website without their permission.

Many manufacturers patrol eBay listings (or have *netenforcers.com* do it for them) searching for images/copied item descriptions that have been used without permission. They report them to eBay through the VeRO program (Verified Rights Owner) and the auction is canceled immediately.

You do not get a refund of any fees if this happens, and a notation is made on your eBay account that you have had a VeRO violation. Too many of these and your account will be suspended.

If you follow the tips in this chapter to take your own pictures, you can make them look just as good as the stock pictures and you do not risk any VeRO issues.

## Help! I Don't Have a Digital Camera!

Don't panic. There are ways around this. First, you can develop regular film at most major drug stores and have the pictures put onto a CD for about $2.50. Or you can wait until they are developed and scan the ones you want to use with a Picture Maker scanner, and then put them onto a CD in the store.

Honestly, digital cameras are so cheap that it is probably worthwhile getting one. Don't bother if you are only going to sell a few items, but if your selling grows beyond that, a digital camera and tripod are a good investment (also tax deductible as a business expense).

If your digital camera is five-years old, don't worry, it will probably be fine for auction photos. If you do want to purchase one, you can now get them quite cheaply. I searched for digital cameras with 2.0 to 2.9 megapixel resolution and 4x zoom on eBay, and I found plenty of *Buy It Now* auctions for under $75. You can always turn around and sell it on eBay if you want to upgrade later on! Entry-level new cameras start around 3 megapixel. If you get one of these, use the lowest resolution setting so you are not wasting space on your memory card.

Choose a brand associated with cameras, rather than one you have never heard of. You will pay more for a Sony, Canon, Nikon, Olympus, Kodak, or Minolta, but the quality will be better. Shop around for the best deals, and always take the opportunity to handle the camera before purchasing (at a retail store, for example) if possible.

# Specifications for an Auction Camera

⊃   One to two megapixels of resolution minimum. You don't need anything higher than this if you are only using the camera for auction photos. If you want to print photos as well, look for three to four megapixels, but shoot auction pictures on the lowest resolution setting.

➲    1.5 inch liquid crystal display (LCD) screen.

➲    Macro (close-up) focus.

➲    Zoom to four inches.

➲    Ability to change white balance settings.

➲    Ability to disable flash.

➲    A tripod.

## Zoom and Macro

Zoom helps you take pictures from a further distance. However, you need to ensure you also use the macro setting (icon looks like a tulip) to get close-up focus. There is no point in getting a close-up with zoom, if the picture is out of focus. You can always crop and enlarge a photo using photo editing software, but it's almost impossible to fix an out of focus image!

## Flash

Automatic flash makes every item look flat and causes distracting glare and shadows. You *must* turn off the automatic flash. *This is a very important step.*

## Resolution Settings

eBay's *Enhanced Picture Services* compresses your picture to 400 pixels on the longest side for a standard size picture, and 800 pixels for a super-sized picture. So, it is pointless shooting a picture with three megapixel resolution unless you are doing some serious cropping. Super-size is not available for pictures smaller than 500 pixels on the shortest side.

eBay recommends at least 1024 pixels (on the shortest side) for all pictures, so they can resize and compress it when you upload.

## JPEG Magic

Your file size cannot exceed 1.2 megabytes (MB) when using *Enhanced Picture Services*, but you shouldn't be above 200K, because of page load times. Most pictures at 1024 pixels use at least 800K of memory. When you save it, change the file type to JPEG. You want the "high" quality setting. This will reduce the required memory for your picture from 800K to about 150K. You will lose a little bit of clarity, but it is not noticeable on the screen (you would only notice the difference if you printed the picture).

*You can use a third-party picture hosting service (like yahoo, or inkfrog.com) instead of eBay's picture services. They usually charge a fee, but it is not "per photo" like eBay charges. These services are usually only worth it if you are listing a lot of auctions. They do not restrict your picture size, so be careful to resize and compress it properly before using one of these services or it will take forever for your picture to load. (And it could be larger than the browser window!) Until you have a bit of experience, stick with eBay's Picture Services.*

## Tripod

Blurry photos are usually caused by infinitesimal movement by your hand when you take the picture, so a tripod is one of the most important photography tools you can own. Generic tripods are available on eBay, and range in price from $5 to $20. Look for tripods at garage sales; I have found good ones for as little as $2.

If you really can't afford a tripod, you will need a table (preferably adjustable height) to rest the camera on.

## What Is White Balance?

The automatic white balance feature on your camera keeps your pictures from looking too orange or too blue, depending on your lighting and environment. However, the camera sometimes gets it wrong (I'm sure you have seen indoor pictures come out with an orange hue). With most cameras, you can keep this from happening by presetting the white balance control to match the type of light you are using, such as tungsten (everyday house-hold bulbs), natural daylight, or fluorescent lights.

On my 5-year old 1.2 megapixel Olympus, I found these settings under *picture*, and then *WB*. Most new cameras will allow you to custom set it (you want 18 percent gray if you have a choice), but even really old ones like mine have different preadjusted settings. Look at the picture in the LCD screen as you select each one, and you will find a setting that will get the colors balanced correctly. For mine, the lightbulb symbol was the best because I was using regular household lightbulbs. Note: Some cameras will call this setting *incandescent*, others will call it *tungsten*. Both terms refer to exactly the same thing—regular household lightbulbs.

## Automatic vs. Manual White Balance

I would like to show the difference between pictures taken with automatic white balance, and those taken with the manually adjusted white balance but, because it is all about color balance, it is impossible to show in a black and white picture.

However, this subject is very important, so go to the resources section of *www.lissamcgrath.com* to see comparison pictures (in color). White balance will make a lot more sense when you see the pictures.

Turning off the flash and adjusting the white balance are two critical steps you *must* take to get professional looking pictures. Even if you do nothing else, these two steps will make your pictures look 100 percent better, which translates into more clicks on your auctions and more bids.

*If you are unsure about any of your camera's settings, consult your manual. (You can download it from the manufacturer's Website.) I find the electronic copy is easier to use because I can go to edit and find, and put in the specific item I am looking for (like white balance), and it will take me straight to that section. This saves a lot of time and searching through the index. www.photonotes.org/dictionary has a great page that explains the icons and acronyms on most cameras.*

## Automatic Exposure

The automatic exposure feature adjusts the exposure to prevent pictures from looking too dark or too light.

If your photos still come out too dark or too light, it is typically because your item or background is very light or dark. You can bring it back to normal with your camera's exposure compensation control (often EV on your camera settings). Choosing a *positive* EV setting will make it lighter and a *negative* one will make it darker.

# Photo Studios

There are many tabletop photo studios on the market. On eBay, most of them sell from $85 to $250. If you plan on setting up an eBay business, it may be worth the investment, but first I recommend following the instructions for the "10 Minute Photo Studio for $10 or less" before you spend money in this area.

There is a more advanced version of the studio setup on Jim's Website (*www.sigma-2.com*) that is ideal for people who want a permanent setup, but this basic version is cheaper and easier for people who are just getting started, or who only have a few items to sell.

## 10-Minute Photo Studio for $10 or Less

The picture on page 50 shows the final setup. As you can see, it is very basic, but very effective.

This is Jim's setup, but I made one for myself that took me about 10 minutes (including deciding which tables and chairs to use).

You will need:

➲    **One sheet of flexible white poster board.** You can get poster board for $0.42 at Wal-Mart, or $0.25 at Hobby Lobby. (Make sure it is not damaged or wrinkled. Arts and craft stores usually take better care of paper storage than Wal-Mart type stores, and are often less expensive.)

⊃   **Two clamps.** You can purchase clamps for approximately $2 to $5 each at Lowes or HomeDepot. I like quick-release, hand-grip clamps (around $4) because they won't damage your furniture and are much easier on your hands. If you already own G-clamps, or something similar, those are fine too.

⊃   **An area next to a well-lit window.** Don't use a window that gets direct sunlight. If you need to shoot pictures at night, put 150-watt light bulbs (not "daylight" bulbs), into two flexible neck desk lamps. Lamps with clips instead of bases work best because you can position them anywhere.

⊃   **A low table.** A coffee table or end table.

⊃   **A high-backed chair.** A dining room or patio furniture chair.

## Four-Step Photo Studio Instructions

1.   Position the chair with the back against the low table.

2.   Clamp the poster board to the table, then curve it up and attach the other end to the back of the chair. (The paper will make a stylized L-shape as shown in the setup picture.)

3.   Position your camera on the tripod in front of the item on the floor (large tripod), or on another table (small tripod).

4.   If you are using lights rather than the window, position them at a 45° angle facing the item on either side of the table.

Now, if you want to play with the shadows, you can place a piece of white card vertically near the left side of the item. This will act as a reflector to fill in the shadows. How much it reflects depends on how close to the object you place it. Play around with it and look at the results. You can also place a shaving or makeup mirror to the right of the item. This will add "sparkle" and highlights to the item.

Even if you don't make the studio, you *must* have a clean, seamless background for your item, and never shoot it with other items (like on a dining room table with other items/wall pictures in the shot) because this clutter detracts from the details of your item.

# Examples of Good and Bad Photos

The picture of Jiminy Cricket on the left shows the problem of taking photos with a cluttered background, automatic flash, and macro not turned on. The image on the right shows how this can be improved by placing your subject alone, and properly adjusting the flash and macro settings.

The next two examples demonstrate how the EV settings and angle of placement can affect item photos. On the left is a picture of a coat taken with a camera where

the settings were not properly adjusted, and the item's placement was poor. The photo on the right is demonstrates a proper use of settings and angle of placement.

## $100 Light Tent vs. a Milk Jug

Now, what if you are selling jewelry or other shiny items? These are typically the worst photographed items on eBay because they reflect light (causing glare). There are two solutions to this. Go out and buy a professional light tent for $100, or use a milk jug.

Yes, you heard me correctly. Next time the kids drain the milk jug, rinse it out and cut off the base. Now, place your item on top of a piece of white card or, contrasting colored fabric. Place the milk jug over the item. Position your two lights pointing at the jug from opposite sides. Now point your camera through the pouring hole (you might need to open this hole up a bit to get the camera lens through) and shoot your picture. You might want to use the timer to take the picture since you can't use a tripod with this technique.

The light is diffused through the plastic of the milk jug so you get enough light for a good picture, but no glare or reflections. You will need to use your zoom and macro settings to get a good close-up. If your camera does not have zoom, cut away more of the bottom of the milk jug until you are the correct distance away from the item. Always make sure you have macro turned on.

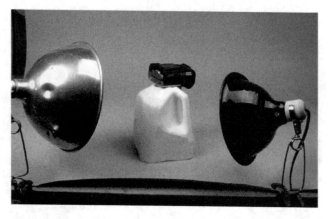

Jewelry is one area where higher resolution pictures are worthwhile. You really want to show as much detail as possible, so fill the image in the screen and shoot with at least one megapixel resolution. If you have a camera that will go higher, this is the time to use it so you can crop down small areas to show details in perfect clarity.

Look at the difference in these two photos of the same watch. The right picture was taken using a light tent, the left picture was without. Which would you bid on?

Jim uses a white plastic bowl he bought at a dollar store. He cut a hole in the side to shoot through (a little easier than through the top, and provides a better angle).

## Light Tent for Large Items

If you are shooting a large item, you can follow the same principles by draping a white sheet over a table. Once again, position your lights on each side of the item (outside the sheet) and you now have a super-sized light tent. You may need higher wattage bulbs to get the light through the fabric though.

# Touch-Ups Without Misrepresentation

If you have photo editing software, you can modify the picture to make it look better. Be careful. you must not make the item look better than it is. Never fix a flaw. This is misrepresentation and will get you into trouble with your buyer, eBay, PayPal and SquareTrade (if you are a member). It will definitely get you negative feedback and a returned item. If you get some glare or unwanted shadows, you can fix those, or add some sparkle to jewelry if it didn't show up in the photo. But, I can't reiterate enough how important it is to make the item look its best *without* making it look better than it actually is.

Make sure your picture is cropped so the image fills the entire picture frame. Rotate it, adjust the colors to get them as close to the actual colors of the item, and make any touch ups before you start your listing. Having the picture completely ready will save you time and effort when you get to that part of the listing process.

*If you don't have photo editing software, eBay's enhanced picture services has limited editing tools. You access this through the* Sell Your Item *form as part of the listing process.*

# More Photography Tips

More of Jim's photography tips can be found on his *About Me* page, or at *www.sigma-2.com*, including a more high-tech version of the photo studio, for those who intend to sell many items and need a permanent setup. Links to his eBay workshops can also be found on this Website. Jim is very active on the photography forums (as *camerajim*) if you need specific help.

# $Q$*uestion* 7

# HOW DO I Build Credibility as a Seller?

## Building Feedback

A high, positive feedback rating is very important as a seller. Imagine having a billboard outside a store where previous customers can make comments about the stores products, service, and integrity. You may well already have feedback as a buyer. Still, it is important to build your "seller" feedback as quickly as possible. I always check a seller's feedback before deciding if I want to purchase from him/her. One or two negatives is usually okay (I will look at the actual comment and follow up by the seller), but a feedback rating below 97 percent makes me seriously reconsider if I want to do business with this person.

### How Do I Actually Do It?

One way is to sell high volume of low cost items, things that sell for a couple of dollars, such as inexpensive trading cards. Have them on short duration (three- to five-day) and/or *Buy It Now* auctions. The object of this isn't to make a high profit, it is to increase your seller feedback so you can make a higher profit on later items. You can often pick up cheap items specific to your local area that collectors will keyword search.

Make sure every transaction is perfect—fast shipping, quick and courteous communication, product exactly as described, and so on. Do not let them have anything to grumble about. The last thing you want at this point is a negative feedback.

## Getting Buyers to Leave Feedback

It is up to the buyer of each transaction to leave feedback as they see fit. Sometimes they forget, so you miss out. I always make a point of posting feedback when I ship an item (and *always* leave positive feedback, even if the customer was difficult, a slow payer, and so on). I don't lie in my feedback, but I make sure to highlight the positive aspects. It is generally better not to leave feedback than leave a negative. Remember, if you leave a buyer a negative feedback, expect the same in return.

Your shipped item e-mail should also include a reminder about feedback (and a link to your other auctions and Website for cross-selling purposes). In additon, include a printed note with your shipped package saying something similar.

## ID Verify

Feedback is very important, but because you are still acquiring seller feedback, you will want to look at other ways of building credibility.

As a PayPal seller, you have had your address verified. Accepting PayPal payments does help the buyer feel more confident about a transaction with you. ID Verify is another very good option.

ID Verify costs $5.00 and is very important if you are selling high-value items (whatever your feedback rating). If you are a smaller seller, it also gives one extra level of credibility. They will run your credit history and ask you two or three questions about it (what is your monthly mortgage payment, and so on) that only you would know the answers to. Once they verify your answers, you can put the ID Verify logo in your auctions, and you will get the ID Verify icon next to your name.

ID Verify is only available to sellers in the United States and U.S. territories at this time. It is valid until you move, or change your name or phone number. At that time, you will have to go through the process again.

Having ID Verify also allows you to sell items using *Buy It Now* without having a 10 feedback rating (as is the usual policy).

If you want to become ID verified, click on *SELL* on the homepage, scroll all the way to the bottom of the page and click on the *Selling Resources* link.

This will take you to the Seller Central page. At the bottom left under Third-Party Resources you will see a link for ID Verify. Click on *sign up now* on the next page and follow the on-screen instructions. Note that you cannot change your eBay username or any contact information for 30 days after becoming ID Verified.

## SquareTrade

Another option is SquareTrade. This is a form of ID verification that goes a step further. If you adhere to their standards, your buyers can have fraud protection under the SquareTrade Buyer Protection program. There are very strict guidelines that you must follow for your buyers to qualify for this. SquareTrade also offers an online dispute resolution (which can also include negative feedback withdrawal).

The Square Trade seller principles include creating listings that are unambiguous regarding the items for sale, shipping and other fees, return policies, shipping times, and so on. Also, the seller must agree to participate in online dispute resolution. You can view the full list of standards on the SquareTrade Website (*www.squaretrade.com*).

The cost for SquareTrade is $7.50 per month (if you pay monthly). If you prepay the first year, you get a 25 percent discount (you pay $67.50 instead of $90). There is a 30 day money-back guarantee, so even if you prepay for the year you can till get your money refunded if you decide (within that time period) that it's not for you.

The two phases of dispute resolution begins with direct negotiation (which is between you and the buyer through the SquareTrade site). If your dispute involves negative feedback, or if direct negotiation doesn't work, you must go forward to mediation. The cost of this is between $19.95 and $29.95, depending on the other services you have signed up for with SquareTrade. I personally think it is well worth $30 to have a negative feedback removed. Go to *www.SquareTrade.com* to find out more.

## BuySafe

If you join BuySafe, you will become bonded up to $25,000. To become a member, you must be approved through their business inspection process. This process evaluates your experience, reputation, track record of honoring commitments, and financial stability, and verifies your identity. They need quite a bit of information from you to do this, but because they are writing a surety bond, you should expect it. They also have a dispute resolution process.

For BuySafe, you pay 1 percent of the final selling price of each item listed with the BuySafe Bond. You are not required to bond every item, and there is no monthly fee. If you only bond four items a year, you only pay for four items a year. Only consider BuySafe if you are selling high-priced items. Go to *www.BuySafe.com* for more information.

# Maintaining a Good Reputation

While all of these techniques will help you build your feedback, it is important to maintain it. Always strive to provide the best transaction the buyer has experienced on eBay. If you treat everyone that way, you will keep your 100 percent feedback rating much longer. Skip McGrath has a 100 percent positive feedback rating and has been selling on eBay for many years. It tells you something about his customer service and integrity that not one person has left him a negative feedback in that time.

# $Q$*uestion* 8

# What Selling Format Should I Use?

It is now time to make your first auction listing. As you work through the next few chapters, you should have your first sale item in front of you. We will be tackling each topic as it comes up on the eBay *Sell Your Item* form, and creating a listing from start to finish.

If you have time, read the entire section first, but if you need to get selling quickly, you can create your eBay listing as you are working through each chapter. Remember, you can change any part of your listing on the final page before you hit *submit*, so you can change your mind on some of the options if you want to.

After you click on *start a new listing*, the next page is titled, *choose a selling format*. There are four options:

- ➲ Sell at online auction.
- ➲ Sell at fixed price.
- ➲ Advertise your real estate.
- ➲ Store Inventory.

If you have a feedback score of less than 10 and are not ID Verified, the *sell at fixed price* option will not be available.

Likewise, if you don't have a store, that option will only be a link to more information about eBay stores.

# Sell Item at Online Auction

This is a traditional "bidding" auction where you list a start-ing price, the buyers place bids and the item is sold to the highest bidder at the end of the auction. You can add the *Buy It Now* option to this type of listing (usually set significantly higher than the starting price), but it will disappear if the bidder chooses to bid rather than *Buy It Now*. If you have a reserve price, the *Buy It Now* option would remain until the reserve is met, and then it will disappear.

# Sell at Fixed Price

This is a *Buy It Now* only auction. You list the price and there is no option for bidding. Once a buyer clicks *Buy It Now*, the auction is completed and the item is sold to that bidder for the price you listed. You have to have a feedback rating of 10 or be ID Verified to list this type of auction. If you want to sell more than one item to different bidders through the same auction (Dutch auction), you must have a feedback score of 30 and be a regis-tered eBay user for at least 14 days, or be ID Verified.

## Best Offer

You can only also use the *Best Offer* option if you are listing a fixed-price Dutch auction. This allows the buyer to submit a price lower than your *Buy It Now* price for your consideration. They can only do this once, and you have the choice to accept it or reject it.

### *Advertise Your Real Estate*

This is a real estate advertisement. It is not an auction. It is designed to get sales leads. Bidding is a request for further in-formation, not a binding contract. I am not going to deal with real estate because it is so highly specific and is not relevant to most buyers. You can find information about it in the eBay help files if you are interested.

# Store Inventory

List an item in your eBay store as a fixed-price, *Buy It Now* auction.

Select your preferred auction type and click *continue*. Most new sellers will use the first option (*online auction*), so if you are unsure, go with that one. This is the option we will be using for the rest of the section.

# $Q$*uestion* 9

# How Should I Choose a Category?

**?**

You are now on the first *Sell Your Item* page, titled *Select Category*.

On your completed items research form, you identified similar items that were successful, and what categories they were listed in. This is your starting point, but there is more research to do.

> *You can use the search box* enter keywords to find a category *and have eBay suggest a category, but where eBay wants to put your item is not necessarily the best place for its visibility. Always do your own research as well.*

## Think Like a Buyer

I expect you already have some experience buying on eBay, so this shouldn't be hard. Think about how you find items on eBay. You likely begin by using a keyword search on the main page. If there are too many results, you might choose a *Matching Category* on the left side bar that is most applicable to your item. Then you can browse through the item titles for an item that interest you.

From this process we can draw two conclusions:

1. The keywords in your title are vitally important.

2. Choosing a category that has other items with the same title keywords is important (the more results a particular category has for the searched keyword, the higher it is in the *Matching Categories* box).

Only the top four to five categories are listed in the *Matching Categories* box, so you *must* make sure your item is in one of those. You want to be in the category/subcategory that is most relevant to your product, but that also has the highest number of items with your keywords in them.

## Keyword Searches

Let's look at an example. Catherine was selling a set of brass-effect PartyLite wall sconces. Prior to listing the items, she began to think of keywords she would use to search for this item:

➲ Candle.

➲ PartyLite.

➲ Candle holder.

➲ Wall sconce.

➲ Brass.

➲ Metal.

➲ Votive.

➲ Tea light.

She started by searching for "candle," because this was clearly the most popular keyword. This gave her 37,757 results. The most popular matching category was "home and garden," with a subcategory of "home décor. The second category was "collectibles," with a subcategory for "decorative collectibles."

Within "home décor," the highest second-level subcategory was "candles/candle holders." Within that subcategory, I would choose "candle holders," then "sconces."

Catherine's item was also a brand name (PartyLite), so she searched that keyword. The top two matching categories were reversed in order, with "collectibles" first, and "home and garden" second. If she were to click on the subcategory for "decorative collectibles," we would clearly see that there was a specific category for PartyLite, and this was where the majority of items with this keyword were listed.

# List in Two Categories

There are two types of bidders to consider: (1) those who are looking for a PartyLite brand item and (2) those who are looking for a wall sconce (not brand specific). This is where the *list item in two categories* option comes in handy. You will have to pay double the fees, but when there are two equally good main categories, like we have with "home and garden" and "collectibles," it is probably worth it. The two categories I would choose include: (1) Home and Garden—Home Décor—Candles, Candle Holders—Candle Holders—Sconces, and (2) Collectibles—Decorative Collectibles—PartyLite—Candle Holders.

You can't use the *list item in two categories* option for a Dutch auction. In these circumstances (or if the value of the item is less than $40), you will have to choose one type of listing. Do a completed items search in each of the categories for items like yours. Scan through the pages and see which category has more successful auctions. That is the category to choose.

Now try the eBay search box on the *sell your item* page and see what eBay recommends. I searched for "PartyLite candle wall sconce" and eBay came up with the same top two categories I had chosen. (The percentage you'll see on the right refers to the number of items with the keywords I specified in each of these categories.) In this instance, I agree with eBay. But there are many times that I identify a better category than the one eBay recommends. Remember, eBay only tells you the percentage of items *listed* in each of the categories. It does not tell you the percentage that ended successfully.

Even if eBay does agree with your choice, your research time has not been wasted. For one thing, you should feel much more confident about listing in that category, because you found it on your own *before* getting a suggestion from eBay.

## Selecting the Category

Okay, let's get back to the *sell your item* page. Start by selecting the main category in the left box. As you make selections, new choices will appear in the next box to the right. You already know the exact category and subcategories you want to use, so this is a very simple process. Imagine how confusing and time-consuming this would be if you hadn't already made your choices though!

## Second Category

This is where you identify your second category if you want to use the *list in two categories* feature. Remember, you will pay double your listing and optional fees. eBay will often suggest a second category for you, but you should stick to your chosen second category if eBay suggests a different one. You will select it in the same way as the first category.

Once you are finished with your second category (if you are using one) click on *continue*.

> *You can come back and remove the second category if, when you get to the end of the listing, you determine that doubling the fees isn't worth it. eBay says listing in a second category boosts bids by 18 percent, so don't bother with this option if it makes your fees exceed 15 percent (to allow for margin errors).*

# Question 10

## How Do I Write a Compelling Title and Subtitle?

After choosing your category, the next page you will come to is *Sell Your Item: Describe Your Item*. This is where you need to use your writing skills.

## Item Title

Your title is the single most important part of your auction. This is the first impression your potential buyers have of your item. A buyer will scan the 40 or so listings on the page for something that catches their eye. How you write your title and subtitle will determine if they click on your auction or just pass you over.

> *Don't use cheesy techniques like L@@K or, BeST dEaL, because even though they are eye-catching, they make you look unprofessional and tacky. This is not the first impression you want to give a buyer!*

# But I'm Not a Writer!

Even if writing is a challenge for you, don't worry. You don't have to be an English major to write an effective title. All you need to do is follow a few basic steps. Much of the work you do now will apply to your item description as well, so it's worth taking your time and doing it properly.

Get a piece of paper and write down as much as you can about the item in short bullet points. Make sure you include both positives and negatives and that you have the item in front of you when you do this. Let's continue using our wall sconce example:

- PartyLite brand.
- Used item.
- Lacquered brass.
- Discontinued style.
- Thick frosted glass candle holder.
- Fits votive or tealight candles.
- Lightweight.
- Pair (opposites).
- Easy to hang (built-in hook).

*If you are selling women's clothes, be aware of the sizing. In your title, you will want to include both the lettered sizing (S, M, L) as well as the numerical sizes (six, eight, 10).*

# Target Audience Profile

Now you need to think about your target audience. Who is this item ideal for? Write down their age, gender, and why it is perfect for them. You may have more than one target audience. For this item, I would identify the following potential three buyers:

1. **Female college students.** Age range 18 to 25 years old. The candle is contained, so there is less risk of fire. Dorms have limited surface space, so being wall-mounted is also a big plus.

2. **Families with children.** This product mounts on the wall way out of kids reach, so you can enjoy the relaxing lighting without worrying about the kids.

3. **A gift for anyone who enjoys candles.** The target buyer, in this case, is an eBay browser looking for a gift. PartyLite is a well-known brand for high-quality candles and accessories.

# Features and Benefits

Get a new sheet of paper and separate it into two columns with the headings Features and Benefits. Look back at your list of bullets. Most of what you have identified will be features. Go through them one at a time, listing the features in the left column, then think of a benefit of that feature.

| Features | Benefits |
| --- | --- |
| *PartyLite Brand* | Known for high-quality products. |
| *Brass lacquered* | Brass style fits any room décor. lacquer prevents tarnish so it looks like new. |
| *Flat hanging hook* | Easy to hang from a small nail. Keeps it flat against the wall. |
| *Frosted glass candle holder* | Diffuses the candle light for a soft romantic glow. |
| *Thick glass* | Won't damage in shipping and won't overheat from candle flame. |
| *Fits tealights or votives* | Use whichever you prefer! |
| *Set of 2* | Instant home design—makes a feature of any wall. |
| *retail $40* | Give as a gift and let them think you paid retail! |

Your title will be made up of features. (You will use the benefits when you write your auction description).

eBay requires you to name the item in the title, so we know we have to use "candle holder," or "sconce." This is where your thesaurus comes in. Look at the features and think of a descriptive word that could go before each one.

Now with these features in mind, we need to think like a bidder again. Go back and look at the keywords you identified during your category research. Consider both the bidder looking for this exact item (a candle wall sconce) and the bidders who may be looking for something similar, but could be interested in this (a candle holder or wall art).

You also have to consider people who search by brand, so we must include the PartyLite brand name. I would suggest "PartyLite, Brass, Wall, Sconce, Candle, Holder."

---

### HOT TIP !

*If you are selling around a holiday, always use the holiday name as a keyword.*

---

You should also try to include trigger words like: amazing, unique, special, sexy, like new, brand new, rare, unusual, hard to find, deal, best value, perfect, NIB (new in box), NWT (new with tags), discontinued, out of print, unopened, sealed, awesome, authentic, and genuine.

Don't forget to look at the titles from your *completed items* research. Take note of words that were repeatedly used in successful auctions. Remember, you only have 55 characters (including spaces), so use the space wisely.

Look at the difference in the following two titles:

---

**PartyLite brass/frosted glass wall sconce candle holder set**

---

> **RARE BRASS WALL SCONCE CANDLE HOLDER**
> **~PartyLite~**
> **Beautiful 2pc set w/frosted glass holder.**
> **PERFECT GIFT!**

If your item doesn't have quite as many keywords to include, you can use white space to make it stand out even more. Consider these identical titles:

> **LIKE NEW GENUINE PRADA BLACK**
> **PURSE HANDBAG**

> **LIKE NEW GENUINE ~~ Prada ~~ BLACK**
> **PURSE HANDBAG**

The second has two spaces between each word and separates the word "Prada" from the rest of the text. If you don't use all 55 characters describing your item, you should use up the remainder by increasing white space.

Write down three to four completely different titles. This will help you think around the item and play with different combinations of words and different triggers. Take the best elements from each of them to make your final title. What you will end up with is a polished, concise, gripping title.

If you are selling at a time of year that makes one target audience more likely to search than others (such as near the start of the new college year) you should tailor your title towards that group. You can use the "shock factor" to your advantage too. Consider the variations on page 70:

---

**COLLEGE ROOM Unique WALL MOUNT PartyLite candle holders**

Clear surfaces—NO FIRE RISK!! RARE PartyLite 2pc set

---

**PROTECT YOUR CHILDREN ~**
**brass wall mount candle holder**
Much safer than tabletop candles—rare PartyLite 2pc set

---

Anyone who searches "Brass," "Wall," "Candle," "Holder," "Children," or "Protect" will see this title. It certainly stands out from the others listings on the page and eBay can't complain because you have listed the item in the title.

Just remember to place keywords in the title, because the subtitle is not searchable unless the buyer checks the *search title and description* box. Use the subtitle to convey more information or benefits about your item. It is particularly important to use a subtitle when you have heavy competition.

## Item Specifics

Depending on your category, you may be offered Item Specifics to select through drop-down menus. I cannot stress enough how important it is to complete these. When a buyer performs a search in certain categories, a *finder* box will appear in the left sidebar for them to narrow down their search results using drop-down menus. If you didn't complete the Item Specifics section (even if your item fits in their search criteria), it will not show up in their results.

*You shouldn't use the symbol \* or " in your title because they have specific search functions. Your keywords will not be found in searches if you use either of these symbols. Instead, I like to use ~*

# $Q$uestion 11

## How Do I Write an Item Description That Sells?

There was a time when you had to know HTML coding to create a professional listing. Thankfully, those days are long gone.

If you already know HTML (HyperText Markup Language), you can click on the second tab, *enter your own HTML*, and have full control over the listing. If, however, you don't know HTML, you should use the *Standard* tab and have eBay take care of the HTML coding for you.

Using the toolbar icons, you can change the font type, size, color, bold, italic, underline, text alignment, add bullets or numbers, or any combination of these options. I recommend you utilize a variety of these throughout your listing, but we are getting ahead of ourselves. First, you need to plan your text.

## Features and Benefits Revisited

Go back to the features and benefits list you made earlier. Now you need to apply the benefits to your listing. You have a lot more space here, so elaborate. Look at the difference in these two opening paragraphs:

## Version 1

Used PartyLite oak leaf pattern wall sconce/candle holder two piece set. Retail price $60. Brass-effect metal is clear lacquered and holds a frosted glass candle holder that fits either a votive or tea light candle. The ring hook mounts it flush against the wall.

## Version 2

### RARE PartyLite BRASS WALL SCONCE CANDLE HOLDERS

Original Retail **$60.00**

#### *Rare, discontinued 2 piece set*

- ⮞ Beautiful ***brass finish*** and ***stylish oak leaf design*** fits any room stylecollege dorm, bedroom, or family living room.

- ⮞ Nontarnish lacquer means they ***never need polishing*** and ***always looks like new***!

- ⮞ ***Thick frosted glass*** holds a ***votive*** or ***tea light*** candle safely and securely, and diffuses the light to ***shed a romantic glow throughout the room.***

- ⮞ PartyLite is the industry leader for high-quality candles and accessories. Give this set as a gift and ***let them think you paid retail!***

- ⮞ Easy to mount flush against any wall using the ring hook (see picture).

- ⮞ ***Matching pair*** (opposites) makes a feature of any wall space.

- ⮞ Set is used, but looks like new (see the ***quality*** in the pictures).

In both examples, I conveyed the same features, but in the second version I included benefits and descriptions that make the item more appealing to my target audience. While the first example is informative, it is not as enthusiastic (and this is important when you try to sell your item).

I used bullets, bold, italic, and underline to make certain features "pop." You should also consider using color. Don't go overboard or your listing will look tacky, but a word or paragraph in a different color here and there makes a big difference.

## Quotations

If you sell a particular item (or type of items) frequently, include a quote from a past buyer. This helps build credibility for you as a seller, as well as for the product you are selling. You may be able to use one of your feedback comments, or an e-mail from the buyer. Make sure to get their permission before using their username if it was from an e-mail. The quote doesn't have to be long:

"I absolutely LOVE my PartyLite candle holder—it's perfect! Finally I can have candles in the living room without worrying about my son!"—sparkles365

## Make It Personal

Address each of the potential buyers you identified earlier and convince them why this is the perfect item they have been looking for. Consider the next few paragraphs:

*Many parents put away their candles because of concerns about young children and fire hazards. But even parents deserve a romantic candlelit evening in!*

*There are no worries about kids (or pets) knocking over these candle holders **they are well out of reach of little fingers and wagging tails**. The frosted glass holder encloses the candle, and also prevents wax from dripping on your carpet!*

*Finally, you can feel safe leaving the room without having to blow out all the candles!*

***This also makes a great gift for a college student.** Dorms are often cluttered, and surface space is rare. Still, all students love to watch movies by candlelight, or enjoy an evening in with that special someone. These wall sconces are the perfect solution.*

Direct words like "you" appeal directly to your audience and make them identify with your product. The tone you use will depend on the item you are selling. Make sure that you are not misrepresenting your item by being overly enthusiastic. I have seen laptop auctions that say "Super fast, 300MHz processor!!!!" This is misleading because 300MHz is incredibly slow, and anyone who doesn't know that will discover it as soon as they receive the item (this brings us back to credibility and feedback).

# The Final Listing

Your first section should begin with a title and catchy paragraph in a larger font than the rest of the listing. Include the item name, retail price, and a quick, one-line description. Don't forget trigger words.

Next, list the features/specifications and benefits. I like using bullets because it looks cleaner, and breaks up the text. The second section appeals directly to your target audience with examples of the item's uses. Include any quotes you have.

The third section should summarize the listing, provide a link to your other auctions, and specify shipping and payment terms. I use headings to separate the information in this section.

The full listing is somewhat long to include in this book, so rather than doing so (where you could not view it in color) I have posted it on my Website (*www.lissamcgrath.com/resources*).

# Checklist

Here are a few tips that you should apply to all listings, no matter what length:

➲ Include *all* specifics of your item, even flaws.

➲ Break up the text by using bullets and extra space between lines.

➲ Use color, bold, italic, and underline to emphasize words and phrases.

➲ Always use a minimum of 14 point text size.

➲ Make sure your browser text size is set to medium before you begin writing your item description.

➲ Clearly state your payment, shipping, and return policies.

➲ Use flat-rate shipping. Use priority mail flat-rate envelopes and boxes when possible, or calculate the shipping to zone four or five (we'll discuss this in shipping and handling).

➲   Use trigger words and descriptions that personalize the item to your target audience(s).

➲   Always link to your other auctions.

# Preview Description

Continue to preview your listing as you are writing. You will need to resize the pop-up window, because it will be smaller than a standard browser window. Make sure that your Internet browser text size is set to medium, because you will be choosing text sizes for your listing that look good in your browser window. If you have the text size set on small, a buyer who looks at your listing (who has it set to the default—medium) sees the text much bigger than you intended, and will have to scroll left and right to view it. Most buyers don't know why this occurs, and will assume you made an error in your listing (and worse, move on to another listing).

## Inserts Menu

To link to your other auctions, click on the *Inserts* drop-down menu on the left of the toolbar and select *Sellers Other Items*.

It will automatically type "Check out my **other items**!" in your listing. You can continue the sentence as I did in my listing, or delete everything but the link and write your own sentence around it.

You may want to reuse some basic text in each of your listings (such as the payment and shipping options). Click on *Inserts* and then *Create Insert*. Copy and paste text from your listing into the box provided and label it for future use. Now when you click on *Inserts* you will see your newly created insert option. This can save you a lot of time.

# $Q$*uestion* 12

## Which Listing Options Should I Choose?

At this stage, you have completed the hardest part of the listing. Now you just need to choose your options and upload your pictures. The page you should be on now is *Pictures & Item Details*. You will need to scroll down this page to get to the other options.

## Starting Price

This is where your completed items research comes in again. From this research, you should know approximately for how much items like yours are selling.

Consider the eBay insertion-fee brackets when setting your starting price. Sellers often start their auctions at $0.99, because it is the highest amount allowed in the lowest fee bracket (it also increases interest because the price is so low). Your starting price should be lower than your expected selling price.

The hardest part is getting the first bid. Buyers browsing through search results notice items that have bids. Once you have one bid, you will likely get more. Lower starting prices can help get these first bids, but you risk having to sell the item at a lower price than you intended. However, you *cannot* bid on your own auction to get this first bid, nor can you have a friend bid for you. This is called "shill bidding," and will get you permanently banned from eBay if you are caught.

The fee bracket cut offs are $0.99, $9.99, $24.99, $49.99, $199.99, and $499.99. If you wanted to start the listing at $55, you should consider $49.99 instead, because it is the highest amount allowed in the lower fee bracket. You would pay an insertion fee of $1.20 to do so, instead of $2.40. This doesn't sound like a big difference, but fees add up quickly.

Continuing with our PartyLite wall sconce example, we know retail was $60. However, we would be happy to sell it for $30, because it is used. In this case, we should list the start price at $24.99.

# Reserve-Price Auctions (RPA)

We briefly discussed reserve-price auctions in the fees section. An RPA allows you to set a low starting price (to generate interest), but reserve the right not to sell the item unless the bidding reaches a certain amount. You pay $1 to $2 for this service, and your listing fee will be based on your reserve price—*not* your starting price. If the item sells, your reserve fee is refunded.

## A Word of Warning About RPAs

Many buyers are wary of reserve-price auctions because they don't know how much they will have to bid to win the item. Sniping is much harder when the auction hasn't past the reserve price, so "bidding wars" are rare.

I have seen many sellers list their reserve price in the item description to combat that. You should consider this technique if you are selling a high-ticket item and significantly undercutting a well-known retail price. But remember you then restrict your potential bidders to buyers who would pay over your listed reserve price. Those who won't pay that amount won't bother bidding (they know they can't meet the reserve, so there would be no point.) This can make it hard to get your first bid.

## Keep Reserves Low

You should keep the reserve as low as possible so the bidder doesn't get bored, and make sure you list "low reserve" in your description. Set the reserve before standard cutoff amounts. For example, a bidder may say their cutoff is $25. So set your reserve at $23 or $24, so they can become the high bidder (and with reserve met, other bidders will be more likely to bid).

Before using an RPA, think about it as a buyer. Would you bid on this item without knowing the reserve price? How many bids would you make before you gave up? Would it make a difference if the reserve price was clearly stated in the auction? Look back at your completed item research forms. How many had reserve prices? Did they sell? How many bids did they receive?

# Reserve-Price Auction vs. *Buy It Now*

Personally, I prefer *Buy It Now* auctions more than RPAs. However, I make an exception to this rule when I have an item that could spark a bidding war and drive up the price. Let's say you have an antique listed and two collectors bidding against each other for it. If you had offered *Buy It Now*, the first collector to see it would have paid that price, and the auction would have ended immediately. With an RPA, you are guaranteed that you won't have to sell it unless it goes above a certain price, but it also gives freedom for bidders to go as high as they want.

# Private Listing

A private listing hides the user ID of the bidders so no one but the seller can see who is bidding on the items. These are used primarily in the "adult" categories, where discretion is important.

Occasionally you see them used for celebrity or high ticket auctions, which is fine. But they should be avoided at all other times.

*A survey conducted by www.AuctionBytes.com revealed that 65 percent of buyers would not bid on a private listing auction.*

# *Buy It Now* Price

If you have a good idea of the item's value, a *Buy It Now* price can be a great tool.

If your listing is a standard online auction format, you can add a *Buy It Now* price to your auction in addition to the original listing price. (Refer to the fees chapter for restrictions and fees.)

If you didn't use a reserve price, then the *Buy It Now* option disappears after the first bid is placed. If you did use a reserve, the *Buy It Now* option will remain until the reserve price is met. At any time until this point, a bidder can use *Buy It Now* and end the auction immediately.

*Buy It Now* is great for well-known items (like video game consoles, laptop computers, printers, and so on). However, if you are selling an antique or a collectible, and you are not an expert, I would not offer *Buy It Now*. An experienced collector may be willing to pay two or three times the price you listed your item for (if they know something about your item that you don't). If you do offer a *Buy It Now* price, you should set it significantly higher than your listing price. If a buyer really wants the item now, they will pay extra for it. This is particularly true around the holiday season, when time is the most critical factor.

# eBay Giving Works

The eBay Giving Works program allows you to donate any percentage of the proceeds from your auction (minimum $10 or 10 percent, whichever is greater) to a participating nonprofit organization. If you donate 100 percent, eBay will donate the listing and final value fees you paid to the same nonprofit.

There are some restrictions, but the donation is tax-deductible, and eBay promotes Giving Works items by placing a ribbon icon next to your auction title. *Charity items only* is also a specific search option. Go to *http://pages.ebay.com/givingworks/index.html* for more information.

# Duration

You have a choice of one-, three-, five-, seven-, or 10-day listings. You pay $0.40 to list a 10-day auction. Your item will determine the duration you choose.

## One-Day Auction

I usually recommend one-day auctions for time-sensitive items (like event tickets), or for auctions held very close to the holidays. Buyers who have left their Christmas shopping to the last minute will be looking for the "ending today" items. With a one-day listing, you will be very visible in this search.

If you have a quantity of a particular item that is highly desirable (always ends with a high bidder at a good price), you can use one-day auctions to increase your selling volume. You can only have 10 identical auctions listed at any one time, so if you are listing three-day auctions, that amounts to 20 maximum per week. One-day auctions would increase that total to 70 auctions a week. Only use this once you are certain the item will sell at every auction, otherwise use Dutch auctions.

## Featuring

We talked about these options in the fees chapter. If you are using *any* feature options, your auction duration should be at least seven days in length, in order to get your money's worth. If you are using homepage feature, it should always be a 10-day listing. I like to offer *Buy It Now* for these items, because you never know when you will rotate onto the homepage. You want to make sure the impulse buyer can get your item now, rather than having to wait for the auction to end (by which time they have usually forgotten about it and moved on).

# Start Time and Schedule Start Time ($0.10)

eBay is officially set to Pacific time. If you are selling from a different time zone, remember this when you set your start time.

If you are incredibly organized, you can save yourself $0.10 by checking *start listing when submitted*. If, however, you are human like the rest of us, just pay the $0.10 and click on *scheduled start time*, to specify an exact start date and time. This will take a lot of pressure off you.

Auctions can be scheduled up to three weeks in advance. Your listing will show up in the Pending Items section of My eBay until the auction begins.

## What Day and Time Should I End My Auction?

Your start time and end time are same. Your auction is most visible when it shows up in the *Time: newly listed* and *Time: ending soonest* search options. It is critical to be part of these search results during peak buying hours.

Ina and David Steiner (publishers of *www.AuctionBytes.com*) conduct a yearly survey of eBay sellers, and address topics such as when to end an auction. If you visit their Website (*http:// auctionbytes.com/cab/abu/y205/m02/abu0137/s03*), you can view the results of each survey. Results are formatted into chart form, and contain information from the last six years.

eBay wants your *start* day, not your *end* day. To work out your start day, and to get more information about good and bad start days, go to David Steiner's auction calendar at: *www.auctionbytes.com*. (Click on *Calendar*, located on the left-hand side bar below *cool tools*.)

*Many experienced buyers are wise to higher selling prices at peak times, and so they search during the days/times that are traditionally considered the worst. Look at the results of your completed items research and see how this corresponds to your specific item/category.*

# Quantity

If you are using the *list in two categories* option, you cannot use a multiple-quantity listing (Dutch auction). However, if you are only selling in one category, you can increase the quantity of identical items you want to list now. Remember you must have a feedback of at least 10 to list a Dutch auction, and you will pay the listing fee multiplied by the quantity you list.

## Item Lots

Selling items in lots (rather than individually) can increase the total price you get for the items. This is particularly true in the clothing categories. A buyer is likely to pay more for a lot of clothes than for individual items, and it is a way for you to sell less desirable items with highly desirable items. Just make sure they are the same sizes! Baby clothes are a particularly good lot item.

Click on the *Lots* tab and input the number of items in the lot. This is also a search option, so make sure you do this if you are selling more than one item.

> *Don't confuse Lots with Dutch auctions. A Dutch auction is a multiple-quantity auction of identical items. Each bidder purchases one item per bid. A Lot auction involves the selling of two or more items (identical or not), and the high bidder gets all of the items listed in the auction. You can have multiple winners in a Dutch auction, but there is only one winner for a Lot auction.*

# Item Location

If this tab is minimized, it will say "zip code not specified." You should click on *change* and input your zip code (or the zip code of where the item is being shipped from).

You can choose to use a custom phrase instead of your city/state. But I don't advise it, because then your auctions will not show up in a search by city/state.

# Question 13

## How Do I Add Pictures to My Auction?

We have discussed how to set up a photo studio, techniques for taking and editing pictures, and so on. Now we need to discuss how to upload them into the auction. There are a number of ways to do this. The easiest is to use eBay's *Picture Services*.

I recommend the *Enhanced Picture Services* because it gives you editing ability, and it is the most compatible for eBay's system. You will need to download the software the first time you use it, but once it is loaded on your computer, you won't need to complete this step again.

## Adding Your Pictures

Remember, your first picture is *free,* and you should *always* include at least one picture in your listing. So don't skip this step, even if you are pressed for time.

The following three bullets correspond to the options for uploading pictures:

➲ **eBay Enhanced Picture Services.**

➲ **eBay Basic Picture Services.** This offers less features than the enhanced service, but no download is needed.

➲ **Your Website Hosting.** You can use this if you have a Website, or a page on Yahoo (or a similar site) where you will be hosting your own pictures.

I recommend Enhanced Picture Services, but I will discuss the other two options as well.

## eBay Enhanced Picture Services

Click on the *Add Pictures* button in the top left box (number one). This will open a window for you to locate your pictures on your computer. Click on *open* once you have selected your first picture. Remember, the first picture will be your gallery/thumbnail picture so use the best one you have. A preview of your picture will appear in the box in the middle of the page and also in the thumbnail box on the left.

> *Enhanced Picture Services can only do basic tasks (contrast, brightness, crop, and rotate), so I prefer to have the image ready when I select it.*

## Basic Picture Services

If you are having trouble with Enhanced Picture Services, and you have already done all of your editing, you can use Basic Picture Services to upload your pictures. Make sure they are under 50KB in size, or the page won't load fast enough and a potential bidder will click away. Remember, not everyone has DSL or cable.

## Your Website Hosting

This is a good option if you are listing many auctions, or you already have your own Website to host your pictures. Yahoo and other sites offer picture hosting for a monthly fee, rather than the "per picture" fee eBay charges. But as a new seller, you should stick with picture services until you have more experience, because your photo will automatically be resized and compressed so it looks professional in your listing.

# Picture Options

When setting up a listing, use as many good pictures as you can to show different details/applications of your product. I think four to six photos is a good number. Always use at least two pictures (one can be stock, but you must always include an actual picture of the item you are selling as well). Your first picture is free, and all additional pictures will cost $0.15 each. We have discussed how important the gallery is, so add $0.35 for that feature. I also highly recommend "supersize." This feature allows your potential bidder to view your item twice the size of the usual auction size (normally 400 × 400 pixels, supersize can expand the size of an image to as large as 800 × 800). This is the most expensive of the picture options at $0.75.

This brings us to a total of $1.25 if two pictures are used, or $1.85 if six pictures are included. However, eBay offers a Picture Pack that includes six pictures, gallery insertion, supersize, and also includes picture show (a slideshow of your pictures that would normally cost an additional $0.25). The Six-Picture Pack is only $1, so it is cheaper, and offers more than the standard option.

# Listing Designer

## Themes

Having selected your picture options, it's time to get creative. eBay has many different borders and backgrounds for you to choose from. Be careful with your selection, because many look tacky and unprofessional. Choose one that reflects your item and category (some category specific designs are available). The *stores* options are good if you can't find a specific one for your item.

# Layout

You have five layout options:

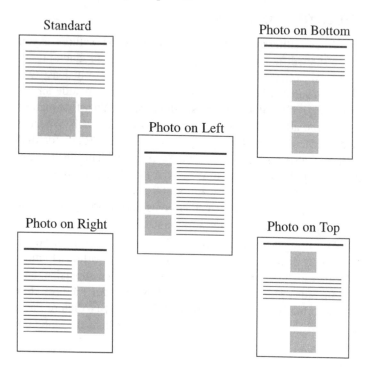

If you are using *supersize* you can only use the standard layout. I like photo on top or photo on left depending on my item. The standard layout is the best option if you are using a lot of pictures because it gives thumbnails for the buyer to click on, which saves space in your listing.

# $Q$*uestion* **14**

# What eBay Features Should I Pay Extra For?

Once you have uploaded your photos, check the boxes for the options you want to use. Be careful—the extra costs do add up. Watch your expected selling price versus fees incurred.

## Gallery ($0.35)

You should never list an item without this feature. If a buyer browses the search results by picture gallery instead of *list view* and your item is not in the gallery, it will not show up.

Many buyers think that listings without the thumbnail picture in *list view* do not have a picture included in the auction so they don't bother clicking on it. The thumbnail only indicates an item is in the gallery, the green camera icon indicates there is a picture in the auction, but it is not listed in the gallery.

## Subtitle ($0.50)

If you added a subtitle, this box will already be checked. You can include one at this point if you didn't earlier, or you can uncheck the box to remove a previously written subtitle.

This isn't essential for all listings, but it is useful when you have a lot of information about your item, or when you want to catch a buyer's eye. At $0.50 it won't break the bank, but you should consider the cost of your item before adding the subtitle. Are there lots of similar items to yours so you need to stand out? If yes, go for it. If not, you probably don't need it.

# Bold ($1)

Always use bold for items that will sell for more than $10 because it makes your listing stand out. Look at the difference in these identical titles:

No formatting:

NIB Epson R300 Printer Ink Cartridges—Free Ship!!!

With bold:

**NIB Epson R300 Printer Ink Cartridges—Free Ship!!!**

The only reason to skip the bold feature is if most other listings in the category are using bold. In that case, you actually make your listing stand out more by *not* using it.

# Border ($3)

The border feature, as the name implies, places a border around your title and photo (which makes the listing "pop"). However, at a cost of $3 you will need to be selling a high-priced item, or be in intense competition with other sellers, to make this worthwhile. If your item will sell for under $20 (and it's not a Dutch auction) I wouldn't recommend this option.

# Highlight ($5)

The highlight is the most expensive option (other than featuring), and should only be used if you are selling a high-priced item. It puts a purple background behind your title and picture. I recommend this for Dutch auctions. This makes it more cost effective (if you are selling one item, you pay $5 for this feature—if you sell five items, it only costs you $1 per item).

# Featuring Options

There are three types of featuring options: Gallery Feature ($19.95), Featured Plus! ($19.95), and Home Page Featured ($39.95/$79.95). I discussed each of them in Question 5, so I won't repeat myself. Just please consider your selling price before choosing any of these high-priced options. These are not refundable if your item does not sell.

# Gift Services ($0.25)

This adds the gift services icon (looks like a wrapped gift) next to your listing. If you select this, check the boxes of services you will offer (*gift wrap/gift card, express shipping,* and/or *ship to gift recipient*).

I don't bother with this feature unless my item is particularly marketable as a gift, or if a holiday is approaching. People use the *gift items* search option mostly around Christmas, so this is the time to use it. Around the beginning of November, I start adding this to my items that could be gifts. Don't bother adding it to items that are missing their original box, or that are obviously used (unless it is a collectible or antique).

# Page Counter

The default is *No counter.* You need a page counter to track the number of page views, so click on *change.* I recommend using the hidden counter so bidders (and other sellers) cannot see how many hits your listing has had.

A bidder who sees only a few page views may decide to wait until the end of the auction to bid, so you don't get the all important first bid early enough in your auction duration. Alternatively, if they see a lot of hits but no bids, they may think there is something they missed wrong with the item and decide not to bid. By using a hidden counter, you can see your page views (through My eBay), but no one else gets to see it.

Once you have selected all of your options, click on *continue.*

# Question15

## What About Payment, Shipping, Handling, and Sales Tax?

At this point, you are almost done with your listing! The page you are currently on should read *Enter Payment and Shipping*.

## Payment Methods

### PayPal

Three out of four buyers prefer to use PayPal, so you should *always* offer this as a payment option. Go to your PayPal account and click on *Auction Tools*. Now, click on *Offer PayPal on All Your Listings (Automatic Logo Insertion)*. This will take you to your auction account management page.

Make sure that it says "on" below both *Automatic Logo Insertion* and *PayPal preferred on eBay*. This will insert the PayPal logos into the *payment methods accepted* section of every listing you create.

## Other Payment Options

You should also offer BidPay, personal check, cashier's check, and money order. Don't accept cash unless the buyer is picking up the item, and always make sure to give them a receipt when this is the case. Refer to the chapter on how to get paid for a listing of the pros and cons associated with each payment method.

# Ship-to Locations

Check the boxes of all the countries you will ship to. Remember, you will need to fill out customs forms for any international countries (including Canada and Mexico). I ship worldwide because items in European countries (particularly England) cost double the U.S. retail price, and their tax rate is much higher (the United Kingdom tax rate is 17.5 percent), so they will often bid higher than U.S. bidders. About 40 percent of my buyers are international.

# Shipping Cost

I recommend flat-rate domestic shipping and instructing international bidders to e-mail you for a quote. This makes it much easier for U.S. bidders to calculate their total cost, and saves you from shipping to an international country for less than your actual cost.

To determine the flat-rate, click on *research rates and services*. Select the package weight and size and click on *continue*. Use the drop-down box under *domestic rates* to select a city. Choose a city far away from you. I choose Seattle, Washington, because I live in Florida. Click *show rates*, and you will see rates for both USPS and UPS services. I use USPS Priority Mail exclusively, because the cost is much lower than comparable services with other carriers.

## Handling Fee

Consider the shipping cost before choosing the handling fee. If the shipping was $20, I would add $3. A good amount for low priced items is $1.50.

Some sellers charge a high shipping rate, but a low listing price for an item. This is because eBay calculates your final value fee on the auction selling price, not including shipping costs. You see this frequently with nondesigner clothing, where there are rarely multiple bidders.

> *Remember, the chart does not show flat-rate box/envelope fees, so you may make a bit of money if you can fit the item into one of these. Also, we calculated the highest cost, so if you ship to a location that is closer, the actual cost will be less.*

Add your handling fee to your total, and then click *show rates* again. Now the totals include your handling fee. Select the box for each service you want to offer, and click *offer services* once you're done. Now the sell your item form is updated to include these choices.

## Shipping Insurance

You should offer this as an option, but not require it unless the item is particularly valuable. Click *change* (next to *not offered),* then click on *rate table* to determine the rate for your item's value. Change the drop-down menu selection to *optional* and input the insurance amount in the box provided.

## Shipping Discounts

I recommend offering combined shipping if your items are not very heavy. Buyers will often browse your other items after their item closes to see if there is anything else they are interested in, so they can combine the shipping.

Check the box next to *Apply a shipping discount when buyer purchases multiple items from me.* Now click on the *shipping discount* link. This will open a new page.

Use the drop down menu to select how many days the purchaser will have to qualify for combined shipping. I usually go with five or seven days depending on the number of active listings I have.

I check the *I will specify shipping discounts later* box, because my policy is 50 percent off the shipping cost for a buyer's second item, and free shipping for the third item. eBay doesn't give me this option, so I specify it in both the item description and in the payment details box.

## Sales Tax

The default is *Seller does not charge sales tax.* You should change this to your local sales tax rate. Click on *sales tax table* and input your local sales tax next to your appropriate state. This will automatically add the sales tax to the total for in-state buyers. You will have to report this quarterly, so make sure to keep track of it. Any tax preparer can help you set this up. They will charge you for the service, but you can expense it on your business taxes.

> *You have to apply for a sales tax ID number (don't worry, it's free). This will also allow you to purchase items for resale tax free. (You can link to your state's sales tax application via my Website).*

## Return Policy

I offer a 14-day unconditional money-back guarantee (less shipping costs). Alternatively, you could say, "I guarantee my items to be exactly as described in my auction, or your money back." Either way, it shows confidence in your items, and often saves you from getting neutral or negative feedback. The second choice will get you less returned items (as long as you are scrupulous about your item descriptions).

Always process refunds the day you receive the returned item. This is easy if they paid with PayPal, but if it was a personal check, make sure it has cleared your bank before sending a refund.

> *Make sure you state that the item must be received in the same condition you originally shipped it. If the buyer thinks they are getting a refund either way, they have no incentive to ensure it is packaged securely. By making this stipulation, you have more chance of it being returned in a relistable condition.*

## Payment Instructions

Specify within how many days payment is required, and explain your combined shipping policy. I usually allow seven days for payment, and additional purchases within those seven days get a 50 percent discount off the second item's shipping, with the third item shipped for free.

## Buyer Requirements

I recommend blocking buyers from countries you don't ship to. This prevents issues with a high bidder who didn't read your terms and conditions. (Particularly important if it is a *Buy It Now* auction.)

You can also block bidders with a negative feedback rating (negative one, negative two, negative three, and lower).

Another option is blocking *Buyers without a PayPal account*. I *never* do this because I don't want to exclude *any* potential buyers, even though I prefer PayPal.

Once you are satisfied, hit *continue*.

# $Q$*uestion* 16

## How Do I Make Sure My Auction Looks Right Before I Submit It?

You are now on the last page! Click *preview how your item will look to buyers* to see how your auction will look.

If you want to make any adjustment, click on *edit preferences* (to the right of each section) to make changes. This is your last chance to modify your listing, so double check everything.

## Listing Fees

Check that the listing fees total what you expected. You can remove any features if the total is too high. Remember, you will need to add the final value fee after the item is sold.

## Proofread

I copy and paste my listing into Microsoft Word and run a spell check. Then I print it out, because it is easier to catch mistakes in printed text. Let someone else read your listing to make sure that you have conveyed the information accurately.

# Spelling

This an interesting point since there are so many international buyers and various spellings for the same words (particularly in British and American English). Use the correct spellings for where your item is located (where you live, where your dropshipper is located, and so on). However, if you choose to sell directly on eBay UK, or other specific international sites, you should use their native spellings.

## But I Don't Know the British spellings!

Don't worry, even I follow this step now if I am selling on the United Kingdom site, and I am originally from England! Copy and paste your text into Microsoft Word and highlight it all. Then go to *tools* and click on *language*, and then *set language*. Change it from *English (U.S.)* to *English (U.K.)*. Also uncheck the *detect language automatically* box. Now run a spell check on the document. The program will identify the misspelled words and suggest the correct spellings for British English. Once that is done, copy and paste it back into your listing (delete the old version first) and you are done.

This is an important because of keyword searches. A British buyer is going to search for keywords with the British spellings, so you want to make sure your item comes up in those searches.

# Check Photos

Preview your listing and confirm that your pictures display as they should (not missing or distorted). You should see a small picture of your item in the top left of the auction (if you are listed in the gallery) and you should see the pictures in your listing. If you see a red "X" with a box around it where the picture should be, upload the picture again.

Make any changes to your listing, upgrade options, and so on, and do a final preview after you have made changes. Have someone else look at it on the screen and give you their opinion.

# eBay Checkout

There is only one more thing to do before you can hit submit. Turn on *eBay checkout*. You will only have to do this once, then it will automatically show on all future listings. Open a new browser window and go to *my eBay*. *C*lick on *preferences* (under the *My Account* heading). Now click on *show* next to *payment from buyers.*

Click on *edit*. This will open a new page.

Under *checkout preferences* check the box *use checkout*. This turns on eBay checkout for all future listings (because we didn't hit submit yet, the current listing is still classified as a future listing.)

Make sure all the boxes are checked under *PayPal preferences*.

Under *buyer edit option* check the box labeled *allow buyer to edit total payment to account for additional costs or discounts*. This enables the buyer to use eBay checkout if they are using your combined shipping service.

Make sure your address is correct for mailed payments, then click *submit*.

Go back to your listing, click *submit* and your item will be listed/scheduled to list at the date and time you specified, and the applicable fees will be charged to your eBay account.

Congratulations! You have just completed your first listing! Your first listing will have taken much longer to create than subsequent listings will take. As you list more and more items, you will become more adept at research, developing keywords for the titles, writing a compelling description, and so on. So don't lose heart if it took you a while to get the first one right. Everyone starts somewhere, and you should be proud of what you have accomplished in the last few hours!

# $Q$*uestion* 17

## How Do I Solve Problems?

Many problems that occur in the eBay process are caused by a lack of communication. Getting the communication right won't make all of your problems go away, but it will make them a lot easier to handle.

## Communicating With Bidders

### My Messages

Most bidders will contact you through the eBay My Messages service that you access through your *My eBay* page (The link is on the left side bar). You should check your My Messages box at least twice a day while you have an active listing. As your auction is nearly complete (within the remaining four hours), check it more frequently, because this is when your item is most visible. Many buyers won't place a bid until they have their question answered. By that time the auction could be finished.

Messages sent to you through the My Messages system are also sent to your e-mail address on file. You can respond to the buyer directly, rather than through My Messages, which can be useful if you need more words than the My Messages system allows. Occasionally a buyer will block you from seeing their e-mail address. In this case, you must respond to them through My Messages.

## Patience Is a Virtue

Always communicate with bidders in a professional manner:

- ➲ Sentences should be well-constructed and text should flow easily.

- ➲ Spell check all e-mails before sending.

- ➲ Address each question or concern logically, and with patience and understanding.

- ➲ *Never* retaliate if you receive a nasty e-mail.

I know it is tough to be nice when you have a difficult buyer, but it will save your feedback. After all, this is only one person.

To help you along, here are a few suggestions for each type of e-mail. I save my standard letters in Microsoft Word on my desktop, so all I have to do is copy and paste into the e-mail and modify as necessary. This saves a lot of time.

## Potential Bidders During the Auction

Start the e-mail with "Dear (username, or real name if you have it)," and thank them for their interest in your item. You should then address each of his or her questions in the order they asked them. Even if the answer is clearly stated in the auction, repeat it again and don't say things like "read the auction description." You need to show your best customer service. Remember, they are deciding to bid or not to bid on your item based on how you respond to them now.

Sign off with "Best regards," or "Happy bidding!" and include your full name, username, and Website URL (if you have one).

## Winning Bidder E-mail

PayPal automatically sends a winning bidder e-mail to your buyer, with a PayPal *pay now* button in it. It is very generic and impersonal, so I suggest you modify it. You can do so by signing in to PayPal and clicking on the *profile* tab at the top right. Next, click on *auctions* (under the *selling preferences* heading). Click on the word *off* beneath *customize end of auction e-mail*. This will take you to a new page where you can modify the end of auction e-mail.

You will see some uppercase text in parentheses. This is a form field that pulls the relevant information for that transaction (buyer's username, auction title, and so on). Add text around these to personalize your e-mail.

In the box, my end of auction e-mail looks like this:

---

Hi {Buyer's USERNAME},

Congratulations! You are the winning bidder of the {TITLE}, {ITEM #}. I hope you will be very pleased with your purchase!

I prefer PayPal, but I also accept BidPay, money orders, cashier's checks, or personal checks. Please contact me if you will be using any of these other payment options.

I ship the same day if payment is received by 2 p.m. If not, I ship the following day. I use USPS Priority Mail, so you should have your item in three to four days from the time it is shipped.

I will e-mail you with the tracking number once your item is shipped. If you have any questions, do not hesitate to contact me.

Don't forget to check out my other auctions (username: lissamcgrath) and my Website: *www.lissamcgrath.com*.

I combine shipping for auction items (50 percent off lower-item shipping, with the third item shipped FREE). If you purchase from my Website, you also get FREE shipping, no matter how many items you purchase.

I appreciate your business!

Best regards,

Lissa McGrath

{SELLER'S USERNAME}

{SELLER'S E-MAIL}

www.lissamcgrath.com

---

I deliberately don't use a link to my auctions, because I want the buyer to go to my Website. Then I can avoid paying eBay fees on a sale. If you don't have a Website, you should include a link to your other auctions in this e-mail. When you are done editing, click *submit*.

## Item Shipped E-mail

PayPal sends another automatic e-mail to the buyer when you print your shipping label. You have the option of including a message, but I prefer to send a separate e-mail once the package is actually in the mail. This is what I recommend:

Dear (*buyer's name*),

Thank you for your payment! Your item will be shipped via Priority Mail tomorrow morning, so you should expect to receive it in three to five business days.

The USPS tracking number is 1234 5678 9102 3456. This has not been scanned by the post office clerks yet, so it won't be available for tracking until tomorrow morning. At that time, you can track the progress of your package by going to: *www.usps.com.*

I have left positive feedback for you and I would appreciate you doing the same. If you have any questions or concerns, please contact me immediately.

Don't forget that you get 10 percent off your first order from *www.lissamcgrath.com*!

Thank you for your business!

Best regards,

Lissa McGrath

(eBay username: *lissamcgrath*)

www.lissamcgrath.com

# Solving Other Problems

## Money-Back Guarantee

The easiest way to solve most problems is to offer a money-back guarantee (excluding shipping). This way, if you get a complaint from a buyer who just won't budge, you can offer the refund and they usually either shut up (because they don't want to ship it back), or they take you up on the offer.

## Getting Your Fees Refunded

After you refund a bidder, you should open an unpaid item dispute with eBay stating it was a mutual withdrawal from the transaction. So long as the buyer acknowledges this when eBay contacts them, you will become eligible for a free relist and have your final-value fee refunded. You can also send a second chance offer to the next highest bidder. And remember, in a mutual withdrawal case, you do not have to wait the usual seven days to file.

## What if I Made a Mistake?

If you were at fault, admit it and apologize. Do whatever you can to make it right. It may cost you more than your profit on the item, but your feedback is going to suffer if you don't. If you sent the wrong item, you should pay for the return shipping and pay for the shipping of the correct item, and send it overnight delivery if possible (find the cheapest price).

## What if I Get a Negative?

eBay requires anyone who tries to leave neutral or negative feedback (when his or her own feedback score is less than 10) to go through a tutorial explaining when negative feedbacks *are* and *are not* appropriate. This does help reduce the petty negatives you often get from new buyers.

If you do get a negative it's not the end of the world. You can post a comment with the negative. If it was because you messed up, admit it. I saw a comment on a negative from one seller that said "He's completely right. I messed up. Doesn't happen often, but it did here." I was so impressed at his honesty, I bid on his item immediately. I would have thought twice if it had said "deadbeat loser bidder. NEVER SATISFIED."

## Nonpaying Bidder

If you encounter a nonpaying bidder, consider sending a message such as the following:

> Dear (*buyer's name*),
>
> You won item # 1234567890, title: (*insert title here*) on (*date*). I noticed that you haven't completed eBay checkout. Please go to: (*insert link to ended auction page*) and click on *Checkout*. If you are having difficulties with this, please let me know so I can help.
>
> If you have already mailed payment, please e-mail me so I know it is on the way. I will ship the item via Priority Mail as soon as I receive payment.
>
> Thank you for your business!
>
> Best regards,
>
> Lissa McGrath
>
> (eBay username: *lissamcgrath*)
>
> www.lissamcgrath.com

## Post-Auction and Business Setup

Now that your auction has ended, there are a few things to do before you are finished with the transaction. We will address these issues in the final chapters. Remember, your buyers will often base their feedback on what you do now.

# $Q$*uestion* 18

## What if My Item Doesn't Sell, or the Buyer Doesn't Pay?

If you were unable to sell your item, or sold it to a buyer who failed to pay, you will not get a refund of your optional-listing fees. However, there are some fee credits you may be entitled to.

## Insertion-Fee Credit

If your item does not sell the first time, you may be able to relist it without paying another insertion fee. To get the credit, you must follow these instructions:

1.  You must relist the item within 90 days of the original auction's close.

2.  Only the first relisting of the item is eligible for the credit.

3.  Both the original auction and the relisted auction must be either a fixed-price auction or regular online auction format (not eBay store inventory or real estate advertisement).

4.  The relisted item's starting price cannot exceed the original auction starting price.

5. If the original auction did not have a reserve price, the relisted auction cannot have one.

6. If the original auction did have a reserve price, the relisted auction may have one, but it cannot exceed the original auctions reserve price.

7. The relisted auction must end with a buyer. If the item doesn't sell again, you will not get the credit for either auction.

8. You may change any descriptions, titles and pictures, provided that you are relisting the exact same item.

To relist an item, go to the ended auction page and click on *relist*. This will take you to the *sell your item* form where you can change the description, title, and so on. You are not eligible for the fee credit if you start a new listing, even if it is the same item.

I strongly recommend you identify why the item didn't sell or reach the reserve price *before* relisting. Did you miscalculate the end day/end time? Did you have a misspelling in your auction title? Did the pictures not load properly? Is there just no market for the item?

# Page Views

Look at your page counter (if you are using the hidden page counter you access this through My eBay). Did you get just a few page views? Or, did you get many page views, but few bids?

## Too Few Page Views

If you didn't get many page views, you should critically look at your gallery picture and auction title. Consider your keywords and check spellings. Also, some of the listing options you didn't choose might be worthwhile (bold, subtitle, and so on).

## Many Page Views but Few Bids

If you are getting the hits (but not the bids) you need to look at the description and photos in your auction. Is there anything you could change to make it more appealing? Is your shipping charge too high? Does it look professional? Is it simply priced too high for your current feedback?

## Completed Item Research Revisited

Redo your completed items research, but this time compare the similar listings to your ended auction. Identify elements of each auction that are good and bad. Then look at your own auction and view it with the same critical eye. Make any changes you see fit before relisting.

You pay the listing fee again when you launch the relisted auction. If the item sells, eBay will refund the listing fee. If it doesn't, you will have paid two listing fees and still have an unsold item. For this reason, the extra research is very important.

# NonPaying Bidders

eBay understands there are people who bid and then don't pay. People sometimes experience buyer's remorse. I have heard some really comical excuses: "My cat walked across my keyboard," "I left my 4 year-old alone for five minutes…" You get the general idea.

## Second Chance Offer

If the high bidder contacts you with an excuse, it is easy to resolve. If you had a "bidding war" at the end of your auction, you can cancel the high bidder's bid and send a *second chance offer* to the second-highest bidder. They would get the item for the highest price *they* bid, not the original highest bidder's price. They are not obligated to take this offer, but most will jump at the chance, particularly if it is still relatively soon after the auction ended.

## Additional Items

If you have more than one item in your inventory, but only listed one in the auction, you can send a second chance offer to any of your bidders (go to the *bid history* and click on *second chance offer*). The advantage of second chance offers is that you are not paying the additional listing fee (as you would in a Dutch auction). You only pay the final-value fee on an accepted second chance offer. This is a great feature to use if there was a bidding war at the end of your auction. You may have four bidders who bid higher than you expected for the item. With the second chance offer, you can capitalize on this and make all four sales without listing another auction.

If you are allowing your high bidder out of their purchasing obligation, make sure you canceled his or her bid, or eBay will charge you the final-value fee for both that item and the second chance offer accepted by any other bidder.

You are not required to use a second chance offer. You can initiate an unpaid item dispute against the nonpaying highest bidder. They have entered into a contract with you, so it is up to you if you want to be nice and allow them out of it. I recommend you try to be accommodating, because they still get to post feedback if you are difficult, they are more likely to give you a negative.

# Dispute Console

The *dispute console* link is on the My eBay page at the bottom left (below *my account*).

## What Is an Unpaid Item Dispute?

If the buyer does not pay (and won't respond to your e-mails) for seven days following the close of the transaction, you should open an unpaid item dispute with eBay. eBay will contact the buyer and attempt to get payment for you. If they are unsuccessful, you can close the case and request a final-value credit. You are also then eligible for a free relist of that item. A buyer is suspended after having three legitimate nonpaying bidder cases filed against them within a short amount of time.

If you initiate a dispute about a nonpaying bidder, and the bidder does not respond to you or eBay (which happens about 80 percent of the time), then the bidder is prevented from leaving feedback for the transaction. However, you can still leave a comment about them. This means that you can give them a negative stating that they were a nonpaying bidder without the fear of getting one in return. Just make sure the case is closed before you do this!

Unfortunately, an e-mail that just says, "I'm not going to pay" is still considered contact. You will get your fees refunded, but the bidder can still leave feedback. At this point a negative or neutral feedback from you will likely get you a similar one in return.

Use your discretion about filing unpaid item disputes. If your listing fee and final value fee were low, you might not want to deal with the hassle, particularly if your feedback is very low (a negative could be devastating in this case).

## Initiating an Unpaid Item Dispute

With a couple of exceptions, you must wait seven days before starting this process, but not longer than 45 days. Get the item number, go to the *dispute console*, and click on *report an unpaid item*.

Follow the prompts to initiate the case. If the buyer does not respond to eBay's communication attempts, you can close the case on the eighth day after it was initiated and request a final-value credit and relist credit. To close the case you have three options:

➲ **We've completed the transaction and we're both satisfied.** Use this if the buyer pays.

➲ **We've agreed not to complete the transaction.** This is what you would use if you are allowing the buyer out of the contract. You will receive a final-value fee credit, and the item is eligible for a relist credit.

➲ **I no longer wish to communicate with or wait for the buyer.** If the buyer does not respond within eight days, or refuses to pay (and is rude about it), this is the option to choose. The buyer receives an *Unpaid Item* strike, you receive a final-value-fee credit, and the item is eligible for a relist credit.

# Question 19

# My Item Sold!
# Now What?

Congratulations! Your customized PayPal "end of auction" e-mail will have been sent to your bidder as soon as the auction closed. You will receive notification from PayPal when they pay. The item will also show up in My eBay under the *items I've sold* section.

## *My eBay* Item's I've Sold

The *items I've sold* part of My eBay shows all the details of the transaction at a glance (buyer's username, selling price, and so on).

To the right of each sold item are six icons. They will be grayed out until the item they correspond to is completed—then they will become bold. This helps you see at a glance exactly what *has* and *has not* been done.

Each icon represents a different part of the transaction:

➲   **Shopping cart.** Buyer has completed "eBay checkout."

➲   **Dollar sign.** Buyer has sent payment. This is turned bold once a PayPal payment is received.

You will have to manually change it (select *mark as payment received* in the drop-down menu) if the buyer sent another form of payment.

➲ **Box.** Item has been shipped (again, use the drop-down menu to select this.)

➲ **Star.** You have left feedback for the buyer.

➲ **Speech bubble.** Buyer has left feedback for you.

➲ **Curved arrow.** Relist status (you can list another identical item, or relist this one if the buyer doesn't pay).

# Packaging and Shipping

There are four reasons I prefer Priority Mail to other services:

1. **Free eBay branded shipping boxes.** You can order free priority mail boxes and envelopes from the U.S. Postal Service (USPS). You must have sold something on eBay within the last 30 days to get eBay branded boxes. (Go to *http://ebaysupplies.usps.com* to order.)

2. **Flat-rate envelopes and boxes.** If your item fits into a flat-rate box or envelope, your shipping cost is the same whatever the weight or U.S. destination. This is a great option if you are selling small, but heavy, items. You can make a bit of money here by charging the buyer the cost for "by weight" Priority Mail, but shipping it flat-rate. Shipping a 5 lb. item from my zip (32508) to Skip's zip (98221) would cost $12.15 via regular Priority Mail. If I can fit it in a flat-rate envelope, it will only be $3.85, or I can use a flat-rate box for $7.70. We profited between $4.45 and $8.30 on that one shipping transaction.

3. **Fast delivery.** You pay less for Priority Mail than UPS Ground, and it often delivers quicker! The USPS usually ships in one to three days. If your destination is the other side of the country, it may take up to four days, but this is still as fast as UPS Ground.

4.  **Free delivery confirmation.** This usually costs $.45, but is free if you purchase the postage online. Always have some form of tracking for every package you send. This protects both you and the buyer.

## Save Money on Packing Materials

Your boxes are free through the USPS, but you also need tape, bubble wrap, and so on.

Go to the category *Business & Industrial—Office, Printing & Supplies—Shipping & Packing Supplies.* There are thousands of items listed. Narrow it down to the particular supplies you need through searching, or the *matching categories* box. These items are much cheaper than retail stores. You also don't have to pay sales tax, and they are shipped directly to your door. Currently, there is a *Buy It Now* auction for 110 feet of bubble wrap for $4.49. Compare that to $3 for 12 ft. at a retail store. You're saving around $22.

Don't forget to keep your receipts. These suppies are all tax deductible business expenses.

## Storage Space

You need somewhere to store shipping supplies. If you don't sell very often, just pick up a few priority mail supplies at your local post office, and get a smaller roll of bubble wrap on eBay.

## Packaging

Whatever box or envelope you use, it is imperative to package the item securely. Think of it as an expensive gift you are shipping to a family member. Use bubble wrap to wrap the item and then polystyrene packing peanuts to fill in gaps in the box. I put the item inside a Priority Mail Tyvek envelope before putting it in the box to help with water resistance, just in case.

## Cross-Selling and Feedback

Before you seal the box, put in a note that says:

> Thank you for your recent eBay purchase. I hope you enjoy your item! I have posted positive feedback for you, and I hope you will do the same. You can access the feedback forum through My eBay. If you have any questions or concerns, please e-mail me immediately so I can help resolve them.
>
> I have other items you may be interested in at my Website: *www.lissamcgrath.com*. You will receive 10 percent off your order! I will also be listing many new items on eBay soon, so please keep checking back!
>
> Enjoy your item!
>
> Lissa McGrath
>
> (eBay username: lissamcgrath)
>
> www.lissamcgrath.com

I included a discount for orders from my Website, but you could use your eBay store, or offer free shipping if they win another auction from you. Customize the letter as much as you want, but *always* include one. It really does make a difference.

## Printing Labels

You can print labels through eBay and pay for postage using your PayPal account. Go to the *items sold* section of My eBay. Click on *print shipping label* in the drop-down menu next to the item's details. This will take you to a PayPal page. Log in and click *continue*.

The next page lists requirements for using the software (Internet Explorer, and so on). Make sure your settings are correct, then click *continue*.

Your address and the buyer's address are listed at the top of the next page. Make sure they are both correct. If you are shipping to a third party via a gift service, you will need to click on *edit* and change the buyer's address.

If you want to use UPS rather than USPS, click on *choose a different shipper* (next to *service type*) and it will take you to a page where you can select UPS. Since I recommend Priority Mail, we will print a USPS label.

1. Select the service type (priority mail, express mail, and so on.)

2. Select the package size.

3. Change the mailing date if necessary. This allows you to print labels in an evening and have them postmarked to ship the following day.

4. Input the item's weight.

5. If you have a specific label printer, you can click on *edit printer settings* and select your label printer. Otherwise, leave this alone.

6. If your item is valued over $250, you must have signature confirmation to be eligible for PayPal's *Seller Protection* so select this option if this applies.

7. Check the box that says *display postage amount on label* if you are offering free shipping (so the buyer can see what you paid). Otherwise, leave it unchecked. Buyers can get annoyed if they see $7.70 on the shipping label, but they paid $12. That is not a good last impression.

8. You can include a message to the buyer, but I don't recommend it.

If your buyer paid for insurance, make sure you add it. Once you are done, click *continue*.

The final page summarizes the shipment details and the funding source to pay for it (PayPal balance, and so on). This is your last chance to change details.

Once you are sure everything is correct, click on *pay and continue*. A pop-up window will show your label (make sure you have pop-ups allowed for this site).

Print a sample label first to make sure you have the right paper, margins, and so on. Then print the actual label and tape it securely to the box. I put clear packing tape over it so it won't get wet if it rains.

In the PayPal transaction details for the shipment (click on the *history* tab, then find the postage transaction and click on *details*) you can reprint the label, or void it entirely if you made a mistake (within 48 hours).

You can also find the delivery confirmation tracking number here. Once you have printed the shipping label, the box icon in My eBay will be bold. Once again, you can select this manually if you didn't use the online label creator.

## Postage Meters

If you are a high-volume seller, you may want to consider a postage meter. Many include a digital scale and automatically calculate your shipping cost and then print it. The bad news is that you have to prepay the postage in a lump sum, and you will pay a monthly fee (around $20) for the rental of the postage meter/scale.

## Same-Day Shipping

Many eBay transactions are impulse buys, so immediate gratification is important. You want feedback comments that praise your "lightning shipping," particularly while you are still building up your rating. I specify that if payment is received by 2 p.m. central time, I will ship it the same day. If not, it will be shipped the following day.

Once you know the item is going to sell (it passes the reserve price), get it packed for shipping. This means all you need to do after the auction closes is create and print the label. Your letter insert is generic, so you can seal the package with that inside before you know who the high bidder will be. This saves time if you have multiple items ending around the same time (as many sellers do). Just make sure you know which item is inside which box!

## Customs Forms for Overseas Transactions

If you are sending an item overseas, you need to complete a customs form (available online at *http://webapps.usps.com/ customsforms*). You must always mark it as merchandise, *not* as a gift, and list the winning bid as the value. Even if the buyer asks you to mark it as a gift, you must politely decline. It is illegal to circumvent customs and duty, and it could get you in a lot of trouble.

If your item is less than 4 lb. you can use Global Priority Mail, which starts at $4. It takes approximately four to seven days to ship with this method. Your other options are Global Express Mail (which arrives within two to four days, but is more expensive), or Airmail (the cheapest option, but takes more than a week).

You can ship to overseas military addresses using regular Priority Mail. This is because the USPS ships to the military mail processing center, and then the military delivers it from there. The one to three days for Priority Mail only applies to getting it to the processing center. Mail can sit for some time (until a pallet is full) before being shipped overseas.

Make sure your buyer is aware of this if they want you to ship to an APO or FPO (an overseas military address that the post office will treat as a U.S. address for pricing and service purposes). Make sure you have a list of the items and both your name and address, and your buyers name and address, inside the package, in case it gets damaged in transit. If the address is overseas, you must complete a customs form as if it were a regular international package, even though it is shipping through a domestic service.

# Leave Positive Feedback

Leave feedback as soon as you ship the item. It doesn't matter how good or bad the transaction was, you must leave positive feedback if you want to build your feedback score. By leaving positive feedback immediately, you are showing confidence in your product.

Once you leave feedback, the star icon will become bold in the *items I've sold* section. The speech bubble icon will change when the buyer leaves feedback for you.

## The Traps of Neutral and Negative Feedback

There are some instances when a negative is appropriate, however you need to decide if it's worth getting one in return. The only time I use a negative is when I have filed an unpaid item dispute, the buyer did not respond, and the case was closed (preventing the buyer from leaving feedback for me). Otherwise, I stick to positives.

# Slow Paying Bidders

Some buyers want immediate gratification, and send PayPal the second they win an auction. Others are a little slower. Be patient. State in your payment terms that payment must be received within a certain number of days or the item will be relisted. If they don't complete the eBay checkout within three days, send them a friendly reminder. If two more days pass, send the non-paying bidder e-mail with a read receipt attached to it (so you can see if the buyer has actually read it). If you have still heard nothing by the seventh day (or whatever day you listed as the last day for receiving payment) try calling them.

## Getting a Buyer's Phone Number

Click on *advanced search,* and select *find contact information* (under the *Member* heading on the left side bar). You need both the buyer's username and the item number for the transaction.

You and the buyer will be e-mailed each other's contact information at the same time. Try calling to see if there is a problem. Again, always be nice. Assume something out of his or her control has occurred, rather than that the customer is a deadbeat.

If you still can't contact them, or he or she still refuse to pay, open an unpaid item dispute.

# Question 20

## How Do I Set Up a Business for Success?

Once you have successfully completed your first eBay sale, it is time to consider how to set up a successful eBay business in order to increase your profits and productivity. In the following pages we will cover the basics for doing so.

## Business License, Sales Tax ID, and Other Initial Steps

To establish your business, you will need to get a business license from your county tax collector. They are usually inexpensive (less than $30). Before you get your license, however, you will need a company name.

### Fictitious Names Register

Be careful when choosing a company name. You must verify that it is not already on your state's Fictitious Name Register (if your state has one). Do a Google search for "fictitious names register" and your state. This should bring up an official site that you can search online. Registration can be usually be completed via the Internet, and will cost around $50. If you don't register, and someone else already has the same company name (or registers it later) you will get some very expensive fines.

## Sales Tax

You have to report and pay sales tax every quarter. Sales tax registration is generally free. Go to your state's main Webpage to find out the regulations that will apply to your business.

Diane Kennedy is an annual *eBay Live* exhibitor who specializes in tax help and information for eBay Business professionals. Her Website, *www.taxloopholes.com*, is worth looking at if you have additional questions regarding sales tax.

## Business Plan

You don't need a comprehensive business plan. But you do need to get your thoughts organized logically. I have compiled a list of considerations you will need to focus on. Take some time and answer each of the following questions thoroughly:

- What items do you want to sell, and why?
- Who is your target audience?
- Will your product appeal to everyone, or only to a select niché market?
- Are there other related products that you can cross sell?
- Where can you obtain your product?
- What shipping carrier will you use, and what is the approximate cost?
- How will you package your product for safe shipping, and how much will your packaging cost?
- How popular is your product? Is it a fad product, or something of enduring nature?
- What are the age and income ranges of your potential customers?

➲ How much competition do you have for your product(s) on eBay?

As your business develops, you will want to make a comprehensive business plan. You can find many books in the library to help you in this process.

## Trading Assistant (TA) Program

This is a way to ease into eBay business. A TA is an experienced seller who sells other people's items on eBay. They take a commission (usually 30 to 40 percent) on each item sold.

This is a great program because you don't need inventory, and if the item doesn't sell, you haven't lost anything. (The buyer pays listing fees.)

There is a search page on eBay where people can find a local TA. To register as a Trading Assistant and be listed on that page, you must have 50 feedback comments at 97 percent positive, and have sold four items in the last 30 days.

## Consignment Stores

A consignment store is a physical location that offers Trading Assistant services. There are many franchise consignment stores across the United States, but small, nonfranchise stores are also doing well.

Skip McGrath has an excellent book titled *How to Start and Run an eBay Consignment Business* (McGraw-Hill, 2006), that details everything you need to know about setting up a successful consignment business. If you want to go this route, this book is an absolute must.

# Increase Profits and Productivity

## eBay Stores

I discussed Dave and his 10 digital cameras at $150 each in the chapter on what eBay will charge. If Dave had an eBay store, he could list a few of his cameras as single-price auctions, and in the item description write, "Need it now? Click here to Buy It Now from my eBay store," and link to his eBay store.

He can charge higher prices in the store, because if someone really wants it immediately, they will pay the higher price. You will get a lot of quick sales by doing this around the holidays. It also helps builds your credibility as a serious seller, rather than someone who is trying to get rid of a substandard item (particularly in the electronics and computer categories).

## Subscription Levels

As with anything, eBay stores don't come free. You must purchase a monthly subscription. There are three levels: basic, featured, and anchor.

➲   A Basic Store ($15.95) gives you five pages to separate your item types into categories, but not much else.

➲   Featured Stores ($44.95) get sales tracking, auction listing services, 10 pages, and better store promotion by eBay.

➲   Anchor Stores ($499.95) are the big dogs. They get much better promotion from eBay, the best sales tracking software, e-mail automation, and so on.

Stay away from both Featured and Anchor subscriptions. For $30 a month, you can get an auction management service with all the features of the anchor stores (except the eBay promotion). If you want to open an eBay store, go for the basic subscription unless you really need the extra pages.

## eBay Stores Fees

To find out what fees are applied to eBay store transactions, go to *http://pages.ebay.com/help/sell/storefees.html*. Here you can find out the optional, listing, and final-value fees for an eBay store. The listing fee is flat-rate, so you can list two items, or 200, for the same listing fee.

## *About Me* Page

This is very important as a new seller. Your *About Me* page should tell the reader something about you, and a lot about your business. This is the only place on eBay that you can list a link to your Website, so make sure you do!

# Cross-Selling and Up-Selling With Multiple Listings

eBay shows four of your other auctions at the bottom of the listing page. Once the auction has ended, they will appear at the top of the page, near the *pay now* button. eBay picks the four items, but you can change them.

Go to your active listing and click *change your cross-promotions* at the top of the page. This allows you to set your own cross-promotion rules, or accept the eBay default rules. Pick items that complement your main item. It can be a loose connection (such as a candle holder and other household décor), or a more specific connection (such as PartyLite candles to go with a PartyLite candle holder). If you did your profile of your potential buyers, it should be fairly easy to determine the items that will have similar target audiences.

# Website

If you are selling high volume, you really need a Website. You can get an excellent template based site for $19.95 a month at *www.citymax.com*. It includes a shopping cart feature (which is often an expensive feature when purchased through an outside source).

What I love about CityMax is the ability to select your current inventory using check boxes. If you run out of an item, just uncheck the box and it will be temporarily removed from your listed inventory. You don't need to do any coding, or make major changes to the site, just check or uncheck a box.

A professionally designed Website costs between $1000 and $10,000, depending on its complexity. Plus you have to pay hosting fees (usually $15 to $20 per month). CityMax gives you customizable templates, shopping cart, hosting, and e-mail accounts for $19.95. This is definitely the way to go.

Your Website name should be easy to spell, and should relate to your business name. At this point, most of the best names have been taken, but there are still some good ones available. Just be creative. You can check *www.register.com* to see if a name is available. I register using *www.wsmdomains.com*, because they only charge $15 per year (whereas other companies charge as much as $30.)

## Auction Automation

If you have a lot of items to list, it is worth investigating automation services such as Zoovy, Andale, and eBay's own service, Turbo Lister. All of these will let you create listings using a much more appealing template than the standard listing designer options. They will let you schedule the start time for free, and you can also upload pictures without using eBay's picture services (which will save you some money).

Turbo Lister is acceptable. It's a free download, and that makes it appealing to new sellers. I recommend you start here before upgrading to a paid service.

*www.Mpire.com* is a new service popular with eBay sellers. It's only $14.95 per month, and that is very reasonable. In the very near future it will be Macintosh compatible as well.

You can get a free 30-day trial of the basic service, or a three-month trial of the professional service, via the link on my Website (*www.lissamcgrath.com*).

# How to Make an Extra $9.95 From Almost Every Auction That Closes

If you have set up an eBay business, you should be working in a niche market. If so, you should be an expert on the subject.

Write an e-book about that topic (if you sell bird accessories, write about how to take care of caged birds). You can go to *www.primopdf.com* and download a FREE tool that will convert any Microsoft document into a pdf. This is the format to send the book so it can't be copied.

In your item shipped e-mail include a tag line such as:

"I have written a book on *X* which you can get from my Website for $9.95! Just input the special offer code: *ebaydeal* to get the reduced price at checkout."

You'd be surprised at the number of buyers who click through. Since it costs you nothing except your time, you make 100 percent profit on this item.

# Where Do I Go From Here?

There are many wholesale and closeout companies that sell in small quantities to eBay sellers. The following are a few good wholesale sites/search engines to find specific products:

- *wholesalecentral.com*
- *closeoutcentral.com*
- *buylink.com*
- *globalsources.com*
- *closeoutsolution.com*
- *maxamwholesale.com*

You can search my favorite (GoWholesale) directly from my Website, *www.lissamcgrath.com*.

Remember, this book doesn't end here. There are many resources (including additional reading suggestions) on my Website as well, to help you succeed with your endeavors.

Good Luck and Have Fun!

# Recommended Reading

I recommend you read Skip McGrath's books. Topics range from selling antiques and collectibles, retail businesses, consignment, and the complete eBay marketing system.

Make sure you also sign up for Skip's newsletter *The Auction Seller's News*. It is completely free. (Links to his books and newsletters are available on my Website.)

I also recommend *Turn eBay Data Into Dollars: Tools & Techniques to Make More Money on Every Transaction*, by Ina Steiner (editor of *AuctionBytes.com*.) Ina is *the* authority on eBay and other auction sites. Her articles are packed with information, so make sure you sign up at *www.auctionbytes.com* (it's also free).

More suggestions are available on my Website.

# Additional Information

## Seller's Checklist

Before you click "submit" on your listing, read it through again and make sure you completed every item on this checklist.

[ ] Use the completed items research form to determine what the item is selling for.

[ ] Take the best photos using the tips in Question 6, then edit and crop them as needed.

[ ] Have the item on hand throughout the listing process.

[ ] Write your profile of potential buyers and why this item is perfect for them.

[ ] Complete the Features and Benefits table.

[ ] Write three to four alternative titles. Pick the best one, or mix a combination to get the best title.

[ ] Write the item description using trigger words and personalizing the item to your potential buyers.

Use bullets, bold, italic, underline, and so on. to make words and phrases "pop." The font size should be at least 14 point.

[ ] Clearly outline your payment, shipping, combined items, and returns policies.

[ ] Use flat-rate shipping. Don't add too much for handling.

[ ] Upload at least two pictures (only one should be stock).

[ ] Always include a picture of the actual item.

[ ] Choose your theme and template.

[ ] Choose additional listing options—bold, highlight, border, and so on.

[ ] Spell check your title and item description.

[ ] Once you are comfortable with the listing, click on *submit*.

## During the auction

[ ] Check My Messages twice a day. Respond to all e-mails with a patient, courteous tone. Always portray a large company, even if it is just you.

[ ] Once you have your first bid (or the reserve is met) you should pack the item carefully with bubblewrap and packing peanuts. Include a note with a feedback request in the packet. Now all you need to do is print the label and hand it to the postal carrier.

# Completed Item Research Form

Main Category and subcategories:

_____

Good title and keywords:

_____

Title and keywords to avoid:

---

| | |
|---|---|
| Bold title? | Yes [ ] No [ ] |
| Highlight? | Yes [ ] No [ ] |
| Border? | Yes [ ] No [ ] |
| Gallery featured? | Yes [ ] No [ ] |
| Featured Plus! | Yes [ ] No [ ] |
| Gallery auction | Yes [ ] No [ ] |
| Number of pictures | _____ |
| Subtitle? | Yes [ ] No [ ] |

Phrases and topics in the subtitle:

---

| | |
|---|---|
| Single-item auction (bidding) | Yes [ ] No [ ] |
| Fixed-price auction (*Buy it Now*) | Yes [ ] No [ ] |
| Dutch auction (Multiple quantity) | Yes [ ] No [ ] |
| *Buy it Now* option in auction format? | Yes [ ] No [ ] |
| Start day: | _____ |
| End day: | _____ |
| Duration: | _____ |
| Start time: | _____ |
| End time: | _____ |
| Number of bids: | _____ |
| Number of page hits | _____ |

Most bids received in which day/time?

---

| | |
|---|---|
| Starting price | _____ |
| Selling price | _____ |
| Reserve price auction? | Yes [ ] No [ ] |
| Reserve price listed in description? | Yes [ ] No [ ] |